THE LOST TRAIL

EDWARD S. ELLIS

1st WORLD
LIBRARY
Literary Society

The Lost Trail

Edward S. Ellis

© 1st World Library, 2007
PO Box 2211
Fairfield, IA 52556
www.1stworldlibrary.com
First Edition

LCCN: 2007930740

Softcover ISBN: 978-1-4218-4815-0
Hardcover ISBN: 978-1-4218-4718-4
eBook ISBN: 978-1-4218-4912-6

Purchase *"The Lost Trail"*
as a traditional bound book at:
www.1stWorldLibrary.com/purchase.asp?ISBN= 978-1-4218-4815-0

1st World Library is a literary, educational organization
dedicated to:

- Creating a free internet library of downloadable ebooks

- Hosting writing competitions and offering book publishing
  scholarships.

1st World Library Literary Society

Giving Back to the World

"If you want to work on the core problem, it's early school literacy."

- James Barksdale, former CEO of Netscape

"No skill is more crucial to the future of a child, or to a democratic and prosperous society, than literacy."

- Los Angeles Times

"Literacy... means far more than learning how to read and write... The aim is to transmit... knowledge and promote social participation."

- UNESCO

"Literacy is not a luxury, it is a right and a responsibility. If our world is to meet the challenges of the twenty-first century we must harness the energy and creativity of all our citizens."

- President Bill Clinton

"Parents should be encouraged to read to their children, and teachers should be equipped with all available techniques for teaching literacy, so the varying needs and capacities of individual kids can be taken into account."

- Hugh Mackay

CONTENTS

CHAPTER I

THE SHADOW

Ye who love the haunts of nature,
Love the sunshine of the meadow,
Love the shadow of the forest,
Love the wind among the branches,
And the rain-shower and the snow-storm,
And the rushing of great rivers.
Listen to these wild traditions.

—HIAWATHA

One day in the spring of 1820, a singular occurrence took place on one of the upper tributaries of the Mississippi.

The bank, some fifteen or twenty feet in height, descended quite abruptly to the stream's edge. Though both shores were lined with dense forest, this particular portion possessed only several sparse clumps of shrubbery, which seemed like a breathing-space in this sea of verdure—a gate in the magnificent bulwark with which nature girts her streams. This green area commanded a view of several miles, both up and down stream.

Had a person been observing this open spot on the afternoon of the day in question, he would have seen a large bowlder suddenly roll from the top of the bank to bound along down the green declivity and fall into the water with a loud splash. This in itself was nothing remarkable, as such things are of frequent occurrence in the great order of things, and the tooth of time easily could have gnawed away the few crumbs of earth that held the stone in poise.

Scarcely five minutes had elapsed, however, when a second bowlder rolled downward in a manner precisely similar to its predecessor, and tumbled into the water with a rush that resounded across and across from the forest on either bank.

Even this might have occurred in the usual course of things. Stranger events take place every day. The loosening of the first stone could have opened the way for the second, although a suspicious observer might naturally have asked why its fall did not follow more immediately.

But, when precisely the same interval had elapsed, and a third stone followed in the track of the others, there could be no question but what human agency was concerned in the matter. It certainly appeared as if there were some *intent* in all this. In this remote wilderness, no white man or Indian would find the time or inclination for such child's play, unless there was a definite object to be accomplished.

And yet, scrutinized from the opposite bank, the lynx-eye of a veteran pioneer would have detected no other sign of the presence of a human being than the occurrences that we have already narrated; but the most inexperienced person would have decided at once upon the hiding-place of him who had given the moving impulse to the bodies.

Just at the summit of the bank was a mass of shrubbery of

sufficient extent and density to conceal a dozen warriors. And within this, beyond doubt, was one person, at least, concealed; and it was certain, too, that from his hiding-place, he was peering out upon the river. Each bowlder had emerged from this shrubbery, and had not passed through it in its downward course; so that their starting-point may now be considered a settled question.

Supposing one to have gazed from this stand-point, what would have been his field of vision? A long stretch of river—a vast, almost interminable extent of forest—a faint, far-off glimpse of a mountain peak projected like a thin cloud against the blue sky, and a solitary eagle that, miles above, was bathing his plumage in the clear atmosphere. Naught else?

Close under the opposite shore, considerably lower down than the point to which we first directed our attention, may be descried a dark object. It is a small Indian canoe, in which are seated two white men and a female, all of whom are attired in the garb of civilization. The young man near the stern is of slight mold, clear blue eye, and a prepossessing countenance. He holds a broad ashen paddle in his hand with which to assist his companion, who maintains his proximity to the shore for the purpose of overcoming more deftly the opposition of the current. The second personage is a short but square-shouldered Irishman, with massive breast, arms like the piston-rods of an engine, and a broad, good-natured face. He is one of those beings who may be aptly termed "machines," a patient, plodding, ox-like creature who takes to the most irksome labor as a flail takes to the sheafs on the threshing-floor. Work was his element, and nothing, it would seem, could tire or overcome those indurated muscles and vice-like nerves. The only appellation with which he was ever known to be honored was that of "Teddy."

Near the center of the canoe, which was of goodly size and straight, upon a bed of blankets, sat the wife of the young man in the stern. A glance would have dissipated the slightest suspicion of her being anything other than a willing voyager upon the river. There was the kindling eye and glowing cheek, the eager look that flitted hither and yon, and the buoyant feeling manifest in every movement, all of which expressed more of enthusiasm than of willingness merely. Her constant questions to her husband or Teddy, kept up a continual run of conversation, which was now, for the first time, momentarily interrupted by the occurrence to which we have alluded.

At the moment we introduce them the young man was holding his paddle stationary and gazing off toward his right, where the splash in the water denoted the fall of the third stone. His face wore an expression of puzzled surprise, mingled with which was a look of displeasure, as if he were "put out" at this manifestation. His eyes were fixed with a keen, searching gaze upon the river-bank, expecting the appearance of something more.

Teddy also was resting upon his paddle, and scrutinizing the point in question; but he seemed little affected by what had taken place. His face was as expressionless as one of the bowlders, save the ever-present look of imperturbable good-humor.

The young woman seemed more absorbed than either of her companions, in attempting to divine this mystery that had so suddenly come upon them. More than once she raised her hand, as an admonition for Teddy to preserve silence. Finally, however, his impatience got the better of his obedience, and he broke the oppressive stillness.

"And what does ye make of it, Miss Cora, or Master

Harvey?" he asked, after a few moments, dipping his paddle at the same time in the water. "Arrah, now, has either of ye saan anything more than the same bowlders there?"

"No," answered the man, "but we may; keep a bright look-out, Teddy, and let me know what you see."

The Irishman inclined his head to one side, and closed one eye as if sighting an invisible gun. Suddenly he exclaimed, with a start:

"I see something now, *sure* as a Bally-ma-gorrah wake."

"What is it?"

"The sun going down in the west, and tilling us we've no time to shpare in fooling along here."

"Teddy, don't you remember day before yesterday when we came out of the Mississippi into this stream, we observed something very similar to this?"

"An' what if we did, zur? Does ye mane to say that a rock or two can't git tired of layin' in bed for a thousand years and roll around like a potaty in a garret whin the floor isn't stiddy?"

"It struck us as so remarkable that we both concluded it must have been caused *purposely* by some one."

"Me own opinion was, ye remember, that it was a lot of school-boys that had run away from their master, and were indulging themselves in a little shport, or that it was the bears at a shindy, or that it was something else."

"Ah! Teddy, there are times when jesting is out of place,"

said the young wife, reproachfully; "and it seems to me that when we are alone in this vast wilderness, with many and many a long mile between us and a white settlement, we should be grave and thoughtful."

"I strives to be so, Miss Cora, but it's harder than paddling this cockle-shell of a canoe up-shtream. My tongue will wag jist as a dog's tail when he can't kape it still."

The face of the Irishman wore such a long, woebegone expression, that it brought a smile to the face of his companion. Teddy saw this, and his big, honest blue eyes twinkled with humor as he glanced upward from beneath his hat.

"I knows yees *prays* for me, Misther Harvey and Miss Cora, ivery night and morning of your blessed life, but I'm afeard your prayers will do as little good for Teddy as the s'arch-warrant did for Micky, the praist's boy, who stole the praist's shirt and give it away because it was lou—"

"*Look!*"

From the very center of the clump of bushes of which we have made mention, came a white puff of smoke, followed immediately by the faint but sharp report of a rifle. The bullet's course could be seen as it skipped over the surface of the water, and finally dropped out of sight.

"What do you say, now?" asked the young man. "Isn't that proof that we've attracted attention?"

"So it saams; but, little dread need we have of disturbance if they always kaap at such a respictable distance as that. Whisht, now! but don't ye saa those same bushes moving? There's some one passing through them! Mebbe it's a shadow, mebbe it's the divil himself. If so, here goes after the imp!"

Catching up his rifle, Teddy discharged it toward the bank, although it was absolutely impossible for his bullet to do more than reach the shore.

"That's to show the old gintleman we are ready and ain't frightened, be he the divil himself, or only a few of his children, that ye call the poor Injuns!"

"And whoever it is, he is evidently as little frightened as you; that shot was a direct challenge to us."

"And it's accepted. Hooray! Now for some Limerick exercise!"

Ere he could be prevented, the Irishman had headed his canoe across stream, and was paddling with all his might toward the spot from which the first shot had been fired.

"Stop!" commanded his master. "It is fool-hardiness, on a par with your general conduct, thus to run into an undefined danger."

Teddy reluctantly changed the course of the boat and said nothing, although his face plainly indicated his disappointment. He had not been mistaken, however, in the supposition that he detected the movements of some person in the shrubbery. Directly after the shot had been fired, the bushes were agitated, and a gaunt, grim-visaged man, in a half-hunter and half-civilized dress, moved a few feet to the right, in a manner which showed that he was indifferent as to whether or not he was observed. He looked forth as if to ascertain the result of his fire. The man was very tall, with a face by no means unhandsome, although it was disfigured by a settled scowl, which better befitted a savage enemy than a white friend. He held his long rifle in his right hand, while he drew the shrubbery apart with his left, and looked forth at the canoe.

"I knew the distance was too great," he muttered, "but you will hear of me again, Harvey Richter. I've had a dozen chances to pick you off since you and your friends started up-stream, but I don't wish to do *that*. No, no, not that. Fire away; but you can do me no more harm than I can you, at this moment."

Allowing the bushes to resume their wonted position, the stranger deliberately reloaded his piece and as deliberately walked away in the wood.

In the meantime, the voyagers resumed their journey and were making quite rapid progress up-stream. The sun was already low in the sky, and it was not long before darkness began to envelop wood and stream. At a sign from the young man, the Irishman headed the canoe toward shore. In a few moments they landed, where, if possible, the wood was more dense than usual. Although quite late in the spring, the night was chilly, and they lost no time in kindling a good fire.

The travelers appeared to act upon the presumption that there were no such things as enemies in this solitude. Every night they had run their boat in to shore, started a fire, and slept soundly by it until morning, and thus far, strange as it may seem, they had suffered no molestation and had seen no signs of ill-will, if we except the occurrences already related. Through the day, the stalwart arms of Teddy, with occasional assistance from the more delicate yet firm muscles of Harvey, had plied the paddle. No attempt at concealment was made. On several occasions they had landed at the invitation of Indians, and, after smoking, and presenting them with a

Edward S. Ellis

few trinkets, had departed again, in peace and good-will.

Not to delay information upon an important point, we may state that Harvey Richter was a young minister who had recently been appointed missionary to the Indians. The official members of his denomination, while movements were on foot concerning the spiritual welfare of the heathen in other parts of the world, became convinced that the red-men of the American wilds were neglected, and conceding fully the force of the inference drawn thence, young men were induced to offer themselves as laborers in the savage American vineyard. Great latitude was granted in their choice of ground—being allowed an area of thousands upon thousands of square miles over which the red-man roamed in his pristine barbarism. The vineyard was truly vast and the laborers few.

While his friends selected stations comparatively but a short distance from the bounds of civilization, Harvey Richter decided to go to the Far Northwest. Away up among the grand old mountains and majestic solitudes, hugging the rills and streams which roll eastward to feed the great continental artery called the Mississippi, he believed lay his true sphere of duty. Could the precious seed be deposited there, if even in a single spot, he was sure its growth would be rapid and certain, and, like the little rills, it might at length become the great, steadily-flowing source of light and life.

Harvey Richter had read and studied much regarding the American aborigines. To choose one of the wildest, most untamed tribes for his pupils, was in perfect keeping with his convictions and his character for courage. Hence he selected the present hunting-grounds of the Sioux, in upper Minnesota. Shortly before he started he was married to Cora Brandon, whose devotion to her great Master and to her husband would have carried her through any earthly tribulations. Although she had not urged the resolution which the young minister had taken, yet she gladly gave up a luxurious home and kind friends to bear him company.

There was yet another whose devotion to the young missionary was scarcely less than that of the faithful wife. We refer to the Irishman, Teddy, who had been a favorite servant for many years in the family of the Richters. Having fully determined on sharing the fortunes of his young master, it would have grieved his heart very deeply had he been left behind. He received the announcement that he was to be a life-long companion of the young man, with an expression at once significant of his pride and his joy.

"Be jabers, but Teddy McFadden is in luck!"

And thus it happened that our three friends were ascending one of the tributaries of the upper Mississippi on this balmy day in the spring of 1820. They had been a long time on the journey, but were now nearing its termination. They had learned from the Indians daily encountered, the precise location of the large village, in or near which they had decided to make their home for many and many a year to come.

After landing, and before starting his fire, Teddy pulled the canoe up on the bank. It was used as a sort of shelter by their gentler companion, while he and his master slept outside, in close proximity to the camp-fire. They possessed a plentiful supply of game at all times, for this was the Paradise of hunters, and they always landed and shot what was needed.

"We must be getting well up to the northward," remarked the young man, as he warmed his hands before the fire. "Don't you notice any difference in the atmosphere, Cora?"

"Yes; there is a very perceptible change."

"If this illigant fire only keeps up, I'm thinking there'll be a considerable difference afore long. The ways yees be twisting and doubling them hands, as if ye had hold of some delightsome soap, spaaks that yees have already discovered a difference. It is better nor whisky, fire is, in the long run, providin' you don't swaller it—the fire, that is."

"Even if swallowed, Teddy, fire is better than whisky, for fire burns only the body, while whisky burns the soul," answered the minister.

"Arrah, that it does; for I well remimbers the last swig I took a'most burnt a hole in me shirt, over the bosom, and they say that is where the soul is located."

"Ah, Teddy, you are a sad sinner, I fear," laughingly observed Mrs. Richter, at this extravagant allusion.

"A *sad* sinner! Divil a bit of it. I haven't saan the day for twinty year whin I couldn't dance at me grandmother's wake, or couldn't use a shillalah at me father's fourteenth weddin'. Teddy *sad*? Well, that is a—is a—a mistake," and the injured fellow further expressed his feelings by piling on the fuel until he had a fire large enough to have roasted a battalion of prize beeves, had they been spitted before it.

Darkness at length fairly settled upon the wood and stream; the gloom around became deep and impressive. The inevitable haunch of venison was roasting before the roaring fire, Teddy watching and attending it with all the skill of an experienced cook. While thus engaged, the missionary and his wife were occupied in tracing the course of the Mississippi and its tributaries upon a pocket map, which was the chief guide in that wilderness of streams and "tributaries." Who could deny the vastness of the field, and the loud call for laborers, when such an immense extent then bore only the name of "Unexplored Region!" And yet, this same headwater territory was teeming with human beings, as rude and uncultivated as the South Sea Islanders. What were the feelings of the faithful couple as their eyes wandered to the left of the map, where these huge letters confronted them, we can only surmise. That they felt that ten thousand self-sacrificing men could be employed in this portion of the country we may well imagine.

As the evening meal was not yet ready, the missionary folded the map and fell to musing—musing of the future he had marked out for himself; enjoying the sweet approval of his conscience, higher and purer than any enjoyment of earth. All at once came back the occurrence of the afternoon, which had been absent from his thoughts for the hour past. But, now that it was recalled, it engaged his mind with redoubled force.

Could he be assured that it was a red-man who had fired the shot, the most unpleasant apprehension would be dissipated; but a suspicion *would* haunt him, in spite of himself, that it was not a red-man, but a white, who had thus signified his hostility. The rolling of the stones must have been simply to call his attention, and the rifle-shot was intended for nothing more than to signify that he was an enemy.

And who could this enemy be? If a hunter or an adventurer, would he not naturally have looked upon any of his own race, whom he encountered in the wilderness, as his friends, and have hastened to welcome them? What could have been more desirable than to unite with them in a country where whites were so scarce, and almost unknown? Was it not contrary to all reason to suppose that a hermit or misanthrope would have penetrated thus far to avoid his brother man, and

Edward S. Ellis

would have broken his own solitude by thus betraying his presence?

Such and similar were the questions Harvey Richter asked himself again and again, and to all he was able to return an answer. He had decided who this strange being might possibly be. If it was the person suspected, it was one whom he had met more frequently than he wished, and he prayed that he might never encounter him again in this world. The certainty that the man had dogged him to this remote spot in the West; that he had patiently plodded after the travelers for many a day and night; that even the trackless river had not sufficed to place distance between them; that, undoubtedly, like some wild beast in his lair, he had watched Richter and his companions as they sat or slumbered near their camp-fire —these, we may well surmise, served to render the missionary for the moment excessively uncomfortable, and to dull the roseate hues in which he had drawn the future.

The termination of this train of thought was the sudden suspicion that this very being was at that moment in close proximity. Unconsciously, Harvey rose to the sitting position and looked around, half expecting to descry the too well remembered figure.

"Supper is waiting, and so is our appetites, be the same token in your stomachs that is in mine. How bees it with yourself, Mistress Cora?"

The young wife had risen to her feet, and the husband was in the act of doing the same, when the sharp crack of a rifle broke the stillness, and Harvey plainly heard and felt the whiz of the bullet as it passed before his eyes.

"To the devil wid yer nonsense!" shouted Teddy, furiously springing forward, and glaring around him in search of the author of the well-nigh fatal shot. Deciding upon the quarter whence it came, he seized his ever-ready rifle, which he had learned to manage with much skill, dashed off at the top of his speed, not heeding the commands of his master, nor the appeals of Mrs. Richter to return.

Guided only by his blind rage, it happened, in this instance, that the Irishman proceeded directly toward the spot where the hunter had concealed himself, and came so very near that the latter was compelled to rise to his feet to escape being trampled upon. Teddy caught the outlines of a tall form tearing hurriedly through the wood, as if in terror of being caught, and he bent all his energies toward overtaking him. The gloom of the night, that had now fairly descended, and the peculiar topography of the ground, made it an exceedingly difficult matter for both to keep their feet. The fugitive, catching in some obstruction, was thrown flat upon his face, but quickly recovered himself. Teddy, with a shout of exultation, sprung forward, confident that he had secured their persecutor at last, but the Irishman was caught by the same obstacle and "floored" even more completely than his enemy.

"Bad luck to it!" he exclaimed, frantically scrambling to his feet, "but it has knocked me deaf and dumb. I'll have ye, owld haythen, yit, or me name isn't Teddy McFadden, from Limerick downs."

Teddy's fall had given the fugitive quite an advantage, and as he was fully as fleet of foot as the Irishman, the latter was unable to regain his lost ground. Still, it wasn't in his nature to give in, and he dashed forward as determinedly as ever. To his unutterable chagrin, however, it was not long before he realized that the footsteps of his enemy were gradually becoming more distant. His rage grew with his adversary's gradual escape, and he would have pursued had he been certain of rushing into destruction itself. All at once he made a second fall, and, instead of recovering, went headlong down into a gully, fully a dozen feet in depth.

Teddy, stunned by his heavy fall, lay insensible for some fifteen or twenty minutes. He returned to consciousness with a ringing sensation in his ears, and it was some time before he could recall all the circumstances of his predicament. Gradually the facts dawned upon him, and he listened. Everything was oppressively still. He heard not the voice of his master, and not even the sound of any of the denizens of the wood.

His first movement was to feel for his rifle, which he had brought with him in his descent, and which he found close at hand. In the act of rising, he caught the sound of a footstep, and saw, at the same instant, the outlines of a person that he knew at once could be no other than the man whom he had been pursuing. The hunter was about a dozen feet distant, and seemed perfectly aware of the Irishman's presence, for he stood with folded arms, facing his pursuer. The darkness prevented Teddy's discovering anything more than his enemy's outline But this was enough for a shot to do its work. Teddy cautiously brought his rifle to his shoulder, and lifted the hammer. Pointing it at the breast of his adversary, so as to be sure of his aim, he pulled the trigger, but there was no response. The gun either was unloaded, or had been injured by its rough usage. The dull click of the lock reached the ear of the target, who asked, in a low, gruff voice:

"Why do *you* seek me? You and I have no quarrel."

"A purty question, ye murtherin' haythen! I'll settle with yees, if yees only come down here like a man. Jist play the wolf and belave me a sheep, and come down here for your supper."

"My quarrel is not with you, I tell you, but with your psalm-singing *master*—"

"And ain't that *meself*?" interrupted Teddy. "What's mine is his, and what's his is mine, and what's me is both, and what's both is me, barring neither one is my own, but all belong to Master Harvey, and Miss Cora, God bless their souls. Don't talk of quarreling wid *him* and being friendly to *me*, ye murtherin' spalpeen! Jist come down here a bit, I say, if ye's got a spick of honor in yer rusty shirt."

"My ill-will is not toward you, although, I repeat, if you step in my way you may find it a dangerous matter. You think I tried to shoot you, but you are mistaken. Do you suppose I could have come as near and *missed* without doing so on *purpose*? To-night I could have brought you and your master, or his wife, and sent you all out of the world in a twinkling. I've roamed the woods too long to miscarry at a dozen yards."

Teddy began to realize that the man told the truth, yet it cannot be said that his anger was abated, although a strong curiosity mingled with it.

"And what's yer raison for acting in that shtyle, to as good a man as iver asked God's blessing on a sunny morning, and who wouldn't tread on one of yer corns, that is, if yer big feet isn't all corns, like a toad's back, as I suspict, from the manner in which ye leaps over the ground."

"*He* knows who I am, and he knows he has given me good cause to remind him of my existence. *He* can tell you, if he chooses; I shall not. But let yourself and him take warning from what you already know."

"And be the same token, let yourself be taking warning. As

sure as I'm the ninth son of the seventh mother, I'll—"

The hunter was gone!

CHAPTER II

THE ADVENTURES OF A NIGHT

The echoing rock, the rushing flood, The cataract's swell, the moaning wood; The undefined and mingled hums— Voice of the desert never dumb! All these have left within this heart A feeling tongue can ne'er impart; A wildered and unearthly flame, A something that's without a name.

—ETTRICK SHEPHERD

With extreme difficulty, Teddy made his way out of the ravine into which purposely he had been led by the hunter. He was full of aches and pains when he attempted to walk, and more than once was compelled to halt to ease his bruised limbs.

As he painfully made his way back to the camp he did a vast deal of cogitation. When in extreme pain of body, produced by a mishap intentionally conceived by another, it is but following the natural law of cause and effect to feel a certain degree of exasperation toward the evil-doer; and, as the Irishman at every step experienced a sharp twinge that ofttimes made him cry out, his ejaculations were neither conceived in charity nor uttered in good-will toward all men.

Edward S. Ellis

Still, he pondered deeply upon what the hunter had said, and was perplexed to know what could possibly be its meaning.

The simple nature of the Irishman was unable to fathom the mystery. He could not have believed even had Harvey Richter himself confessed to having perpetrated a crime or a wrong, that the minister had been guilty of anything sufficient to give cause of enmity. The strange hunter whom they had unexpectedly encountered several times, must be some crack-brained adventurer, the victim of a fancied wrong, who, most likely, had mistaken Harvey Richter for another person.

What could be the object in firing at the missionary, yet taking pains that no harm should be inflicted? That was another impenetrable mystery; but, let it be comprehensible or not, the wrathful servitor inwardly vowed that, if the man crossed the path of himself or his master again, and the opportunity offered, he should shoot him down as he would a wild animal.

In the midst of his absorbing reverie, Teddy suddenly paused and looked around him. He was lost. Shrewd enough to understand that to attempt to extricate himself would only lead into a greater entanglement, from which it might not be possible to escape at all, he wisely concluded to remain where he was until daylight. Gathering a few twigs and leaves, with his well-stored "punk-box" he soon started a small fire, by the light of which he collected a sufficient quantity of fuel to last until morning.

Few scenes of nature are more impressive than a forest at night. That low deep roar, born of silence itself—the sad sighing of the wind—the tall, column-like trunks, resembling huge sentinels keeping guard over the mysteries of ages—the silent sea of foliage overhead, that seems to shut in a world of its own—all have an influence, peculiar, irresistible and sublime.

The picket upon duty is a prey to many an imaginary danger. The rustling of a leaf, the crackling of a twig, the flitting shadows of the ever-changing clouds, are made to assume the guise of a foe, endeavoring to steal upon him unawares. Again and again Teddy was certain he heard the stealthy tread of the strange hunter, or some prowling Indian, and his heart throbbed violently at the expected encounter. Then, as the sound ceased, a sense of his utter loneliness came over him, and he pined for his old home in the States, which he had so lately left.

A tremulous wail, which came faintly through the silence of the boundless woods, reminded him that there were other inhabitants of the solitude besides human beings. At such times, he drew nearer to the fire, as a child would draw near to a friend to shun an imaginary danger.

But, finally the drowsy god asserted himself, and the watcher passed off into a deep slumber. His last recollection was a dim consciousness of hearing the tread of something near the camp-fire. But his stupor was so great that he had not the inclination to arouse himself, and with his face buried in the leaves of his bushy couch, he quickly lost cognizance of all things, and floated off into the illimitable realms of sleep— Sleep, the sister of Death.

He came out of his heavy slumber from feeling something snuffing and clawing at his shoulder. He was wide awake at once, and all his faculties, even to his anger, were aroused.

"Git out, ye owld sarpent!" he shouted, springing to his feet. "Git out, or I'll smash yer head the same as I smashed the assassin's, barring I didn't do it!"

The affrighted animal leaped back several yards, as lightly as a shadow. Teddy caught only a glimpse of the beast, but could plainly detect the phosphorescent glitter of his angry eyes, that watched every movement. The Irishman's first proceeding was to replenish the fire. This kept the creature at a safe distance, although he began trotting around and around, as if to seek some unguarded loophole through which to compass the destruction of the man who had thus invaded his dominions.

The tread of the animal resembled the rattling of raindrops upon the leaves, while its silence, its gliding motion, convinced the inexperienced Irishman of the brute's exceedingly dangerous character. His rifle was too much injured to be of use and he could therefore only keep his precocious foe at a safe distance by piling on fuel until the camp-fire burned defiantly.

There was no more sleep for Teddy that night. He had received too great a shock, and the impending danger was too imminent for him to do any thing but watch, so long as darkness and the animal remained. Several times he thought there was evidence of the presence of another beast, but he failed to discover it, and finally believed he had been mistaken.

It was a tiresome and lonely occupation, this incessant watching, and Teddy had recourse to several expedients to while away the weary hours. The first and most natural was that of singing. He trolled forth every song that he could recall to remembrance, and it may be truly said that he awoke echoes in those forest-aisles never before heard there. As in the pauses he heard the volume of sound that seemed quivering and swaying among the tree-trunks, like the confined air in an organ, he was awed into silence.

"Whist, ye son of Patrick McFadden; don't ye hear the responses all around ye, as if the spirits were in the organ loft, thinkin' ye a praist and thimselves the choir-boys. I belaves, by me sowl, that ivery tree has got a tongue, for hear how they whispers and mutters. Niver did I hear the likes. No more singin', Teddy my darlint, to sich an audience."

He thereupon relapsed into silence, but it was only momentary. He suddenly looked out into the darkness which shrouded the still watchful beast from sight, and exclaimed:

"Ye owld shivering assassin, out there, did yees ever hear till how Tom O'Reilly got his wife? Yees never did, eh? Well, then, be aisy now, and I'll give yees the truths of the matter.

"Tom was a great, rollicking boy, that had an eye gouged out at the widow Mulloney's wake, and an ugly cut that made his mouth six inches wide: and, before he got the cut, it was as broad as yer own out there. Besides, his hair being of a fire's own red, you may safely say that he was not the most beautiful young man in Limerick, and that there wasn't many gals that were dying of a broken heart for the same Tom.

"But Tom thought a mighty sight of the gals and a great deal more of Kitty McGuire, that lived close by the brook as yees come a mile or two out of this side of Limerick. Tom was possessed after that same gal, and it only made him the more determined when he found that Kitty didn't like him at all. He towld the boys he was bound to have her, and any one who said he wasn't would get his head broke.

"There was a little orphan girl, whose father had gone to Ameriky and whose mother was dead, that was found one night, years before, in front of old Mrs. McGuire's door. She was about the same age as Kitty, and the owld woman took her out of kindness and brought them up together. She got to be jist as ugly a looking a gal as Tom was a man. Her hair was redder than his, and her face was just that freckled that yees couldn't tell which was the freckle and which was the skin itself. And her nose had a twist, on the ind of it, that made one think it had been made for a corkscrew, or some machine that you bore holes with.

"This gal, Molly Mulligan, used to encourage Tom to come to the house, and was always so mighty kind to him that he used to kiss and shpark her by way of compinsating her for her trouble. She used to take this all *very* well, for she was a great admirer of Tom's, and always spoke his praise. But Tom didn't make much headway with Kitty. It wasn't often that he could saa her, and when he did; she was mighty offish, and was sure to have the owld woman present, like a dumb-waiter, to be sure. She come to tell him at length that she didn't admire his coming, and that he would greatly plaise her if he would make his visits by staying away altogether. The next time Tom went he found the door locked, and, after hammering a half-hour, and being towld there was no admittance, he belaved it was meant as a kind hint that his company was not agreeable. Be yees listening, ye riptile?

"Tom might have stood it very well, if another chap hadn't begun calling on Kitty about this time. He used to go airly in the evening, and not come out of the house till after midnight, so that one might belave his visits were welcome. This made Tom feel mighty bad, and so he hid behind the wall and waylaid the chap one night. He would have killed the chap, his timper was so ruffled, if the man hadn't nearly killed him afore he had the chance. He laid all night in the gutter, and was just able to crawl home next day, while the fellow went a-courting the next night, as if nothing had happened.

"Tom begun to git melancholy, and his mouth didn't appear quite as broad as usual. Molly Mulligan thought he had taken slow poison and it was gradually working through his system; but he could ate his pick of praties the same as iver. But Tom felt mighty bad; that fact can't be denied, and he went frequently to consult with a praist that lived near this ind of Limerick, and who was knowed to cut up a trick or two during his lifetime. When Tom came out one day looking bright and cheery, iverybody belaved they had been conspiring togither, and had hit on some thavish trick they was to play on little Kitty McGuire.

"When the moon was bright, Kitty used to walk to Limerick and back again of an evening. Her beau most likely went with her, but sometimes she preferred to go alone, as she knowed no one would hurt a bonny little gal as herself. Tom knowed of these doings, as in days gone by he had jined her once or twice. So one night he put a white sheet around him as she was coming back from Limerick, and hid under the little bridge over the brook. It was gitting quite late, and the moon was just gone down, so, when she stepped on the bridge, and he came out afore her, she gave one shriek, and like to have fainted intirely.

"'Make no noise, or I'll ate ye up alive,' said Tom, trying to talk like a ghost.

"'What isht yees want?' she asked, shaking like a leaf, 'and who are yees?'

"'I'm a shpirit, come to warn ye of your ill-doings.'"

"'I know I'm a great sinner,' she cried, covering her face with her hands; 'but I try to do as well as I can.'"

"'Do you know Tom O'Reilly?' he asked, loud enough to be

heard in Limerick. 'You have treated him ill.'"

"'That I know I have,' she sobbed, 'and how can I do him justice?'"

"'He loves you.'"

"'I know he does!'"

"'He is a shplendid man, and will make a much bitter husband than the spalpeen that ye now looks on with favor.'"

"'Shall I make him my husband?'"

"'Yis; if ye wish to save yourself from purgatory. If the other man marries yees, he'll murder yees the same night.'"

"'Oh!' shrieked the gal, as if she'd go down upon the ground, 'and how shall I save meself?'"

"'By marrying Tom O'Reilly.'"

"'Is that the only way?'"

"'Ay. Does yees consint?'"

"'I do; I must do poor Tom justice.'"

"'Will ye marry him this same night?'"

"'That I will.'"

"'Tom is hid under this bridge; I'll go down and bring him up, and he'll go to the praist's with yees. Don't ye shtir or I'll ate yees.'"

"So Tom whisked under the ind of the bridge, slipped off the sheet, all the time kaaping one eye cocked above to saa that Kitty didn't give him the shlip. He then came up and spoke very smilingly to the gal, as though he hadn't seen her afore that night. He didn't think that his voice was jist the same.

♦

"Kitty didn't say much, but she walked very quiet by his side, till they came to the praist's house at this ind of Limerick. The owld fellow must have been expecting him, for before he could knock, he opened the door and let him in. The praist didn't wait long, and in five minutes he towld them they were man and wife, and nothing but death could iver make them different. Tom gave a regular yell that made the windys rattle, for he couldn't kaap his faalings down. He then threw his arms around his wife, gave her another hug, and then dropped her like a hot potato. For instead of being Kitty McGuire, it was Molly Mulligan! The owld praist wasn't so bad after all. He had told Kitty and Molly of Tom's plans, and they had fixed the matter atween thim.

"Wal, the praist laughed, and Tom looked melancholier than iver; but purty soon he laughed too, and took the praist's advice to make the bist of the bargain. Whisht!"

Teddy paused abruptly, for he heard a prolonged but faint halloo. It was, evidently, the call of his master, and indicated the direction of the camp. He replied at once, and without thinking one moment of the prowling brute which might be upon him instantly, he passed beyond the protecting circle of his fire, and dashed off at top of his speed through the woods, and ere long reached the camp-fire of his friends. As he came in, he observed that Mrs. Richter still was asleep beneath the canoe, while her husband stood watching beside her. Teddy had determined to conceal the particulars of the conversation he had held with the officious hunter, but he related the facts of his pursuit and mishap, and of his futile attempt to make his way back to camp. After this, the two seated themselves by the fire, and the missionary was soon asleep. The adventures of the night, however, affected Teddy's nerves too much for him even to doze, and he therefore maintained an unremitting watch until morning.

At an early hour, our friends were astir, and at once launched forth upon the river. They noted a broadening of the stream and weakening of the current, and at intervals they came upon long stretches of prairie. The canoe glided closely along, where they could look down into the clear depths of the water, and discover the pebbles glistening upon the bottom. Under a point of land, where the stream made an eddy, they halted, and with their fishing-lines, soon secured a breakfast which the daintiest gourmand might have envied. They were upon the point of landing so as to kindle a fire, when Mr. Richter spoke:

"Do you notice that large island in the stream, Cora? Would you not prefer that as a landing-place?"

"I think I should."

"Teddy, we'll take our morning meal there."

The powerful arms of the Irishman sent the frail vessel swiftly over the water, and a moment later its prow touched the velvet shore of the island. Under the skillful manipulations of the young wife, who insisted upon taking charge, their breakfast was quickly prepared, and, one might say, almost as quickly eaten.

They had now advanced so far to the northward that all felt an anxiety to reach their destination. Accordingly no time was lost in the ascent of the stream.

The exhilarating influence of a clear spring morning in the forest, is impossible to resist. The mirror-like sparkle of the water that sweeps beneath the light canoe, or glitters in the dew-drops upon the ashen blade; the golden blaze of sunshine streaming up in the heavens; the dewy woods, flecked here and there by the blossoms of some wild fruit or flower; the cool air beneath the gigantic arms all a-flutter with the warbling music of birds; all conjoin to inspire a feeling which carries us back to boyhood again—to make us young once more.

As Richter sat in the canoe's stern, and drank in the influence of the scene, his heart rose within him, and he could scarcely refrain from shouting. His wife, also, seemed to partake of this buoyancy, for her eyes fairly sparkled as he glanced from side to side. All at once Teddy ceased paddling and pointed to the left shore. Following the direction of his finger, Richter saw, standing upon the bank in full view, the tall, spare figure of the strange hunter. He seemed occupied in watching them, and was as motionless as the tree-trunks behind him—so motionless, indeed, that it required a second scrutiny to prove that it really was not an inanimate object. The intensity of his observation prevented him from observing that Teddy had raised his rifle from the canoe. He caught the click of the lock, however, and spoke in a sharp tone:

"Teddy, don't you dare to—"

His remaining words were drowned in the sharp crack of the piece.

"It's only to frighten him jist, Master Harvey. It'll sarve the good purpose of giving him the idee we ain't afeard, and if he continues his thaiving tricks, he is to be shot at sight, as a shaap-stalin' dog, that he is, to be sure."

"You've hit him!" said his master, as he observed the hunter leap into the woods.

"Thank the Lord for that, for it was an accident, and he'll l'arn we've rifles as well as himself. It's mighty little harm, howiver, is done him, if he can travel in that gay style."

"I am displeased, for your shot might have taken his life, and—but, see yonder, Teddy, what does that mean?"

Close under the opposite bank, and several hundred yards above them was discernible a long canoe, in which was seated at least a dozen Indians. They were coming slowly down-stream, and gradually working their way into the center of the river. Teddy surveyed them a moment and said:

"That means they're after us. Is it run or fight?"

"Neither; they are undoubtedly from the village, and we may as well meet them here as there. What think you, dear wife?"

"Let us join them, by all means, at once."

All doubts were soon removed, when the canoe was headed directly toward them, and under the propulsion of the many skillful arms, it came like a bird over the surface of the waters. A few rods away its speed was slackened, and, before approaching closer, it made a circuit around the voyageurs' canoe, as if the warriors were anxious to assure themselves there was no decoy or design in this unresisting surrender.

Evidently satisfied that it was a *bona fide* affair, the Indians swept up beside our friends, and one of the warriors, stretching out his hands, said:

"Gib guns me—gib guns."

"Begorrah, but it would be mighty plaisant to us, if it would be all the same to yees, if ye'd be clever enough to let us retain possission of 'em," said Teddy, hesitating about complying with the demand. "They might do ye some injury, ye know, and besides, I didn't propose to—"

"Let them have them," said Richter. The Irishman reluctantly obeyed, and while he passed his rifle over with his left hand, he doubled up his right, shaking it under the savage's nose.

"Ye've got me gun, ye old log of walnut, but ye hain't got me fists, begorrah, but, by the powers, ye shall have them some of these fine mornings whin yer eyes want opening."

"Teddy, be silent!" sharply commanded the missionary.

But the Indians, understanding the significance of the Irishman's gestures, only smiled at them, and the chief who had taken his gun, nodded his head, as much as to say he, too, would enjoy a fisticuff.

When the whites were defenseless, one of the savages vaulted lightly into their canoe, and took possession of the paddle.

"I'm highly oblaiged to ye," grinned Teddy, "for me arms have been waxin' tired ever sin' I l'arned the Injin way of driving a canoe through the water. When ye gets out o' breath jist ax another red-skin to try his hand, while I boss the job."

The canoes were pulled rapidly up-stream. This settled that the whites were being carried to the village which was their original destination. Both Harvey and his wife were rather pleased than otherwise with this, although the missionary would have preferred an interview or conversation in order to make himself and intentions known. He was surprised at the knowledge they displayed of the English language. He overheard words exchanged between them which were as easy to understand as much of Teddy's talk. They must be, therefore, in frequent communication with white men. Their location was so far north that, as Richter plausibly inferred, they were extensive dealers in furs and peltries, which must be disposed of to traders and the agents of the American Fur and Hudson Bay Companies. The Selkirk or Red river settlement also, must be at an easily accessible distance.

It may seem strange that it never occurred to the captives that the savages might do them harm. In fact, nothing but violence itself would have convinced the missionary that such was contemplated. He had yielded himself, heart and soul, to his work; he felt an inward conviction that he was to accomplish great good. Trials and sufferings of all imaginable kinds he expected to undergo, but his life was to be spared until the work was accomplished. Of that he never experienced a moment's doubt.

Our readers will bear in mind that the period of which we write, although but a little more than forty years since, was when the territory west of the Mississippi was almost entirely unknown. Trappers, hunters and fur-traders in occasional instances, penetrated into the heart of the mighty solitude. Lewis and Clarke had made their expedition to the head-waters of the Columbia, but the result of all these visits, to the civilized world, was much the same as that of the adventurers who have penetrated into the interior of Africa.

It was known that on the northwest dwelt the warlike Blackfeet, the implacable foes of every white man. There, also, dwelt other tribes, who seemed resolved that none but their own race should dwell upon that soil. Again, there were others with whom little difficulty was experienced in bartering and trading, to the great profit of the adventurous whites, and the satisfaction of the savages; still, the shrewd traders knew better than to trust to Indian magnanimity or honor. Their reliance under heaven, was their tact in managing the savages, and their own goodly rifles and strong arms. The Sioux were among the latter class, and with them it was destined that the lot of Harvey Richter and his wife should be cast.

The Indian village was reached in the course of a couple of hours. It was found to be much larger than Richter could have anticipated. The missionary soon made known his character and wishes. This secured an audience with the leading chief, when Harvey explained his mission, and asked permission for himself and companions to settle among them. With the ludicrous dignity so characteristic of his people, the chief deferred his reply until the following day, at which time he gave consent, his manner being such as to indicate that he was rather unwilling than otherwise.

That same afternoon, the missionary collected the dusky children of the forest together and preached to them, as best he could, through the assistance of a rude interpreter. He was listened to respectfully by the majority, among whom were several whom he inferred already had heard the word of life. There were others, however, to whom the ceremony was manifestly distasteful. The hopeful minister felt that his Master had directed him to this spot, and that now his real life-work had begun.

CHAPTER III

THE JUG ACQUAINTANCES

With that dull, callous, rooted impudence, Which, dead to shame and every nicer sense, Ne'er blushed, unless, when spreading Vice's snares, He stumbled on some virtue unawares.

—CHURCHILL

A YEAR has passed since the events recorded in the preceding pages, and it is summer again. Far up, beside one of those tributaries of the Mississippi, in the western portion of what is now the State of Minnesota, stands a small cabin, such as the early settlers in new countries build for themselves. About a quarter of a mile further up the stream is a large Sioux village, separated from the hut by a stretch of woods through which runs a well-worn footpath. This arrangement the young missionary, Harvey Richter, preferred rather than to dwell in the Indian village. While laboring with all his heart and soul to regulate these degraded people, and while willing to make their troubles and afflictions his own, he still desired a seclusion where his domestic cares and enjoyments were safe from constant interruption. This explains why his cabin had been erected at such a distance from his people.

Every day, no matter what might be the weather, the missionary visited the village, and each Sabbath afternoon, when possible, service was held. This was almost invariably attended by the entire population, who now listened attentively to what was uttered, and often sought to follow the counsels uttered by the good man. A year's residence had sufficed to win the respect and confidence of the Indians, and to convince the faithful servant that the seed he had sown was already springing up and bearing fruit.

About a mile from the river, in a dense portion of the wood, are seated two persons, in friendly converse. But a glance would be required to reveal that one of these was our old friend Teddy, in the most jovial and communicative of moods. The other, painted and bedaubed until his features were scarcely recognizable, and attired in the gaudy Indian apparel, sufficiently explains his identity. A small jug sitting between them, and which is frequently carried to the mouth of each, may disclose why, on this particular morning, they seemed on such confidential terms. The sad truth was that the greatest drawback to Harvey Richter's ministrations was his own servant Teddy. The Indians could not understand why he who lived constantly with the missionary, should be so careless and reckless, and should remain "without the fold," when the good man exhorted them in such earnest language to become Christians. It was incomprehensible to their minds, and served to fill more than one with a suspicion that all was not what it should be. Harvey had spent many an hour with Teddy, in earnest, prayerful expostulation, but, thus far, to no purpose.

For six months after the advent of the missionary and his wife, nothing had been seen or heard of the strange hunter, when, one cold winter's morning, as the former was returning from the village through the path, a rifle was discharged, and the bullet whizzed within an inch or two of his eyes. He might have believed it to be one of the Indians, had he not secured a fair look at the man as he ran away. He said nothing of it to his wife or Teddy, although it occasioned him much trouble and anxiety of mind.

A month or two later, when Teddy was hunting in the woods, and had paused a moment for rest, a gun was discharged at him, from a thick mass of undergrowth. Certain that the unknown hunter was at hand, he dashed in as before, determined to bring the transgressor to a personal account. Teddy could hear him fleeing, and saw the agitation of the undergrowth, but did not catch even a glimpse of his game.

While prosecuting the search, Teddy suddenly encountered an Indian, staggering along with a jug in his hand. The savage manifested a friendly disposition, and the two were soon seated upon the ground, discussing the fiery contents of the vessel and exchanging vows of eternal friendship. When they separated it was with the understanding that they were to meet again in a couple of days.

Both kept the appointment, and since that unlucky day they had encountered quite frequently. Where the Indian obtained the liquor was a mystery, but it was an attraction that never failed to draw Teddy forth into the forest. The effect of alcoholic stimulants upon persons is as various as are their temperaments. The American Indian almost always becomes sullen, vindictive and dangerous. Now and then there is an exception, as was the case with the new-made friend of Teddy. Both were affected in precisely a similar manner; both were jolly.

"Begorrah, but yees are a fine owld gintleman, if yer face

does look like a paint-jug, and ye isn't able to lay claim to one-half the beauty meself possesses. That ye be," said Teddy, a few moments after they had seated themselves, and before either had been affected by the poisonous liquid.

"I loves you!" said the savage, betraying in his manner of speech a remarkable knowledge of the English language. "I think of you when I sleep—I think of you when I open my eyes—I think of you all the time."

"Much obleeged; it's meself that thinks and meditates upon your beauty and loving qualities all the time, barring that in which I thinks of something else, which is about all the time—all the same to yer honor."

"Loves you very much," repeated the savage; "love Mister Harvey, too, and Miss Harvey."

"Then why doesn't ye come to hear him preach, ye rose of the wilderness?"

"Don't like preaching."

"Did yees ever hear him?"

"Neber hear him."

"Yer oughter come; and that minds me I've never saan ye around the village, for which I axes yees the raison?"

"Me ain't Sioux—don't like 'em."

"Whinever yees are discommoded with this jug, p'raps it wouldn't be well for yees to cultivate the acquaintance of any one except meself, for they might be dispoused to relave yees of the article, when yees are well aware it's an aisy matter for us to do that ourselves. Where does yees get the jug?"

"Had him good while."

"I know; but the contents I mean. Where is it ye secures the vallyble contents?"

"Me get 'em," was the intelligent reply..

"That's what I've been supposing, that yees was gitting more nor your share; so here's to prevint," remarked Teddy, as he inverted the jug above his head. "Now, me butternut friend, what 'bjections have yees to that?"

"All right—all be good—like Miss Harvey?"

Teddy stared at the savage, as if he failed to take in his question.

"Like Miss Harvey—good man's squaw—t'ink she be good woman?"

"The loveliest that iver trod the airth—bless her swate soul. She niver has shpoken a cross word to Teddy, for all he's the biggest scamp that iver brought tears to her eyes. If there be any thing that has nigh fotched this ould shiner to his marrowbones it was to see something glistening in her eyes," said the Irishman, as he wiped his own. "God bliss Miss Cora," he added, in the same manner of speech that he had been wont to use before she became a wife. "She might make any man glad to come and live alone in the wilderness wid her. It's meself that ought to be ashamed to come away and l'ave her alone by herself, though I thinks even a wild baste would not harm a hair of her blissid head. If it wasn't for this owld whisky-jug I wouldn't be l'aving her," said

Teddy, indignantly.

"How be 'lone?—Mister Harvey dere."

"No, he isn't, by a jug-full—barring the jug must be well-nigh empty, and the divil save the jug, inny-how; but not until it's impty."

"Where Mr. Harvey go, if not in cabin?" asked the savage, betraying a suspicious eagerness that would have been observed by Teddy upon any other occasion.

"To the village, that he may preach and hould converse wid 'em. I allers used to stay at home when he's gone, for fear that owld thaif of a hunter might break into the pantry and shtail our wines—that is, if we had any, which we haven't. Blast his sowl—that hunter I mane, an' if iver I cotch him, may I be used for a flail if I don't settle *his* accounts."

"When Mister Harvey go to village?"

"Whin he plaises, which is always in the afternoon, whin his dinner has had a fair chance to sittle. Does ye take him for a michanic, who goes to work as soon as he swallows his bread and mate?" said the Irishman, with official dignity.

"Why you not stay with squaw?"

"That's the raison," replied Teddy, imbibing from the vessel beside him. "But you will plaise not call Miss Cora a *shquaw* any more. If ye does, it will be at the imminent risk of havin' this jug smashed over yer head, afther the whisky is all gone, which it very soon will be if a plug isn't put into your mouth."

"Nice woman—*much* good."

"You may well say that, Mister Copperskin, and say nothing else. And it's a fine man is Mister Harvey, barring he runs me purty close once in a while on the moral quishtion. I'm afeard I shall have to knock under soon. If I could but slay that thaif of a hunter that has been poking around here, I think I could go the Christian aisy; but whin I thinks of *that* man, I faals like the divil himself. They's no use tryin' to be pious whin *he's* around; so pass the jug if ye don't mane to fight meself."

"He bad man—much bad," said the savage, who had received an account of him from his companion.

"I promised Master Harvey not to shoot the villain, excipt it might be to save his life or me own; but I belave if I had the chance, I'd jist conveniently *forgit* me promise, and let me gun go off by accident. St. Pathrick! *wouldn't* I like to have a shindy wid the sn'akin, mean, skulkin' assassin!"

"Does he want kill you?"

"Arrah, be aisy now; isn't it me master he's after, and what's the difference? Barring I would rather it was meself, that I might sittle it gintaaly wid him;" and Teddy, "squaring" himself, began to make threatening motions at the Indian's head.

"Bad man—why not like Mr. Harvey?" said the savage, paying no attention to Teddy's demonstrations.

"There yees has me. There's something atween 'em, though what it might be none but Mr. Harvey himself knows, less it mought be the misthress, that I don't belave knows a word on it. But what is it yer business, Mr. Mahogany?"

"Mebbe Mr. Harvey hurt him some time—do bad with him,"

added the Indian, betraying an evident interest in the subject.

"Begorrah, if yees can't talk better sinse nor that, ye'd bist put a stopper on yer blab. The idaa of me master harming any one is too imposterous to be intertained by a fraa and inlightened people—a fraa and inlightened people, as I used to spell out in the newspapers at home. But whisht! Ye are a savage, as don't know anything about Fourth of July, an' all the other affections of the people."

"You dunno what mebbe he done."

"Do ye know?" asked Teddy, indignantly.

"Nebber know what he do—how me know?"

"Thin what does ye mane by talking in that shtyle? I warns ye, there's some things that can't be passed atween us and that is one of 'em. If ye wants to fight, jist you say that again. I'm aching for a shindy anyhow: so now s'pose ye jist say that again." And Teddy began to show unmistakable signs of getting ready.

"Sorry—didn't mean—feel bad." "Oh blarney! Why didn't ye stick to it, and jist give me a chance to express meself? But all's right; only, be careful and don't say anything like it again, that's all. Pass along the jug, to wash me timper down, ye know."

By this time Teddy's ideas were beginning to be confused, and his manner maudlin. He had imbibed freely, and was paying the consequences. The savage, however, had scarcely taken a swallow, although he had made as if to do so several times. His actions would have led an inexperienced person to think that he was under the influence of liquor; but he was sober, and his conduct was feigned, evidently, for some purpose of his own. Teddy grew boisterous, and insisted on constantly shaking hands and renewing his pledges of eternal friendship to the savage, who received and responded to them in turn. Finally, he squinted toward the westering sun.

"I told Mr. Harvey, when I left, I was going to hunt, and if I expects to return to-day, I thinks, Mr. Black Walnut, we should be on our way. The jug is intirely impty, so there is no occasion for us to remain longer."

"Dat so—me leave him here."

"Now let's shake hands agin afore we rise."

The shaking of hands was all an excuse for Teddy to receive assistance in rising to his feet. He balanced himself a moment, and stared around him, with that aimless, blinking stare peculiar to a drunken man.

"Me honey, isn't there an airthquake agitatin' this solitude?" he asked, steadying himself against a sapling, "or am I standing on a jug?"

"Dunno—mebbe woods shake—feel him a little—earth must be sick," said the savage, feigning an unsteadiness of the head.

"Begorrah, but it's ourselves that's the sickest," laughed Teddy, fully sensible of his sad condition. "It'll niver do to return to Master Harvey in *this* shtyle. There'd be a committee of investigation appointed on the spot, an' I shouldn't pass muster excipt for a whisky-barrel, och hone!"

"Little sick—soon be well—then shoot."

"I wonder now whether I could howld me gun straight

enough to drop a buffler at ten paces. There sits a bird in that tree that is grinning at me. I'll t'ach him bitter manners."

The gun was discharged, the bullet passing within a few inches of the head of the Indian, who sprung back with a grunt.

"A purty good shot," laughed Teddy; "but it *would* be rayther tiresome killing game, being I could only hit them as run behind me, and being I can't saa in that direction, I'll give over the idaa; and turn me undivided attention to fishing. Ah, divil a bit of difference is it to the fish, whin a worm is on the right ind, whether a drunken man or a gintleman is at the other."

The Indian manifested a readiness to assist every project of the Irishman, and he now advised him to fish by all means, urging that they should proceed to the river at once. But Teddy insisted upon going to a small creek near at hand. The savage strongly demurred, but finally yielded, and the two set out, making their way somewhat after the fashion of a yoke of oxen.

Upon reaching the stream, Teddy, instead of pausing upon the bank, continued walking on until he was splashing up to his waist in water. Had it not been for the prompt assistance of the Indian, the poor fellow most probably would have had his earthly career terminated. This incident partially sobered Teddy, and made him ashamed of his condition. He saw the savage was by no means so far gone as himself, and he bewailed his foolishness in unmeasured terms.

"Who knows but Master Harvey has gone to the village, and Miss Cora stands in the door this minute, 'xpacting this owld spalpaan?"

"No go till arternoon," said the savage.

"What time might it be jist now?"

"'Tain't noon yit—soon be—bimeby."

"It's all the same; I shan't be fit to go home afore night, whin I might bist stay away altogether. And you, Mr. Copperskin, was the maans of gittin' me in this trouble."

"*Me* make you drink him?" asked the savage. "You not ax for jug, eh? You not want him?"

"Yes, begorrah, it was me own fault. Whisky is me waikness. Its illigant perfume always sits me wild fur it. Mister Harvey was belaving, whin he brought me here, that I wouldn't be drinking any of the vile stuff, for the good rais'n that I couldn't git none; but, what'll he say now? Niver was I drunker at Donnybrook, and only once, an' that was at me father's fourteenth weddin'."

"Don't want more?"

"NO!" thundered Teddy. "I hope I may niver see nor taste another drop so long as I live. I here asserts me ancient honor agin, an' I defy the jug, ye spalpeen of a barbarian what knows no better." Teddy's reassertion of dignity was very ludicrous, for a tree had to support him as he spoke; but he evidently was in earnest.

"Neber gib it—if don't want it."

"They say an Indian never will tell a lie to a friend," said Teddy, dropping his voice as if speaking to himself. "Do you ever lie, Mr. What's-your-name?"

"No," replied the savage, thereby uttering an unmitigated falsehood.

"You give me your promise, then, that ye'll niver furnish me anither drap?"

"Yis."

"Give me yer hand."

The two shook hands, Teddy's face, despite its vacant expression, lighting up for the time with a look of delight.

"Now I'll fish," said Teddy. "P'raps it is best that ye l'ave these parts; not that I intertains inmity or bad-will toward you, but thin ye know—hello! yees are gone already, bees you?"

The Indian had departed, and Teddy turned his attention toward securing the bait. In a few moments he had cast the line out in the stream and was sound asleep, in which condition he remained until night set in.

CHAPTER IV

AN OMINOUS RENCOUNTER

"I will work him To an exploit now rich in my device,
Under the which he shall not choose but fall."

The sun passed the meridian, on that summer day in 1821
and Harvey Richter, the young missionary, came to the door
of his cabin, intending to set forth upon his walk to the
Indian village. It was rather early; the day was pleasant and
as his wife followed him, he lingered awhile upon the steps,
loth to leave a scene of such holy joy.

The year which the two had spent in that wilderness had
been one of almost unalloyed happiness. The savages,
among whom they had come to labor, had received them
more kindly than they deemed it right to anticipate, and had
certified their esteem for them in numberless ways. The
missionary felt that a blessing was upon his labor.

An infant had been given them, and the little fellow brought
nothing but gladness and sunlight into the household. Ah!
none but a father can tell how precious the blue-eyed image
of his mother was to Harvey Richter; none but a mother can
realize the yearning affection with which she bent over the

sleeping cherub; and but few can enter into the rollicking pride of Teddy over the little stranger. At times, his manifestations were fairly uproarious, and it became necessary to check them, or to send him further into the woods to relieve himself of his exuberant delight.

Harvey lingered upon the threshold, gazing dreamily away at the mildly-flowing river, or at the woods, through which for a considerable distance, he could trace the winding path which his own feet had worn. Cora, his wife, stood beside him, looking smilingly down in his face, while her left hand toyed with a stray ringlet that would protrude itself from beneath her husband's cap.

"Cora, are you sorry that we came into this wild country?"

The smile on her face grew more radiant, as she shook her head without speaking. She was in that pleasant, dreamy state, in which it seems an effort to speak—so much so that she avoided it until compelled to do so by some direct question.

"You are perfectly contented—happy, are you?"

Again the same smile, as she answered in the affirmative by an inclination of the head.

"You would not change it for a residence at home with your own people if you could?"

The same sweet denial in pantomime.

"Do you not become lonely sometimes, Cora, hundreds of miles away from the scenes of your childhood?"

"Have I not my husband and boy?" she asked, half

reproachfully, as the tears welled up in her eyes. "Can I ask more?"

"I have feared sometimes, when I've been in the village, that perhaps you were lonely and sorrowful, and often I have hurried my footsteps that I might be with you a few moments sooner. When preaching and talking to the Indians, my thoughts would wander away to you and the dear little fellow there. And what husband could prevent them?" said Harvey, impulsively, as he drew his wife to him, and kissed her again and again.

"You must think of the labor before you."

"There is scarcely a moment of my life in which I don't, but it is impossible to keep you and him from my mind. I am sorry that I am compelled to leave you alone so often. It seems to me that Teddy has acted in a singular manner of late. He is absent every afternoon. He says he goes hunting and yet he rarely, if ever, brings anything back with him."

"Yesterday he returned shortly after you left, and acted so oddly, I did not know what to make of him. He appeared very anxious to keep me at a distance, but once he came close enough for me to catch his breath, and if it did not reveal the fumes of liquor then I was never more mistaken in my life."

"Impossible! where could he obtain it?"

"The question I asked myself and which I could not answer; nevertheless his manner and the evidence of his own breath proved it beyond all doubt to my mind. You have noticed how set he is every afternoon about going away in the woods. Such was not his custom, and I think makes it certain some unusual attraction calls him forth."

"What can it all mean?" asked the missionary of himself. "No; it cannot be that he brought any of the stuff with him and concealed it in the boat. It must have been discovered."

"Every article that came with us is in this house."

"Then some one must furnish him with it, and who now can it be?"

"Are there not some of your people who are addicted to the use of liquor?"

"Alas! there are too many who cannot withstand the tempter; but I never yet heard of an Indian who knew how to *make* it. It is only when they visit some of the ports, or the Red river settlement, that they obtain it. Or perhaps a trader may come this way, and bring it with him."

"And could not Teddy have obtained his of such a man?"

"There has been none here since last autumn, and then those who visited the village had no liquor with them. They always come to the village first so that I could not avoid learning of their presence. Let me see, he has been away since morning?"

"Yes; he promised an early return."

"He will probably make his appearance in the course of an hour or so. Watch him closely. I will be back sooner to-day, and we shall probe this matter to the bottom. Good-by!"

Again he embraced his wife, and then strode rapidly across the Clearing in the direction of the woods. His wife watched his form winding in and out among the trees, until it finally disappeared from view; and then, waiting a few moments

Edward S. Ellis

longer, as if loth to withdraw her gaze from the spot where she had last seen him, she finally turned within the house to engage in her domestic duties.

The thrifty housewife has seldom an idle moment on her hands, and Cora passed hither and thither, performing the numerous little acts that were not much in themselves, but collectively were necessary, if not indispensable, in her household management. Occasionally she paused and bent over her child, that lay sleeping on the bed, and like a fond mother, could not restrain herself from softly touching her lips to its own, although it was at the imminent risk of awaking it.

An hour passed. She went to the door and looked out to see whether Teddy was in sight; but the woods were as silent as if they contained no living thing. Far away over the river, nearly opposite the Indian village, she saw two canoes crossing the stream, resembling ordinary-sized water-birds in the distance. These, so in harmony with the lazy, sunshiny afternoon, were all that gave evidence that man had ever invaded this solitude.

Cora Richter could but be cheerful, and, as she moved to and fro, she sung a hymn, one that was always her husband's favorite. She sung it unconsciously, from her very blithesomeness of spirits, not knowing she was making music which the birds themselves might have envied.

All at once her ear caught the sound of a footstep, and confident that Teddy had come, she turned her face toward the door to greet him. She uttered a slight scream, as she saw, instead of the honest Hibernian, the form of a towering, painted savage, glaring in upon her.

Ordinarily such a visitor would have occasioned her no

surprise or alarm. In fact, it was rare that a day passed without some Indian visiting the cabin—either to consult with the missionary himself, or merely to rest a few moments. Sometimes several called together, and it often happened that they came while none but the wife was at home. They were always treated kindly, and were respectful and pleased in turn. During the nights in winter, when the storm howled through the forest, a light burned at the missionary's window, and many a savage, who belonged often to a distant tribe, had knocked at the door and secured shelter until morning. Ordinarily we say, then, the visit of an Indian gave the young wife no alarm.

But there was something in the appearance of this painted sinewy savage that filled her with dread. There was a treacherous look in his black eyes, and a sinister expression visible in spite of vermilion and ocher, that made her shrink from him, as she would have shrunk from some loathsome monster.

As the reader may have surmised, he was no other than Daffodil or Mahogany, who had left Teddy on purpose to visit the cabin, while both the servant and his master were absent. In spite of the precaution used, he had taken more liquor than he intended; and, as a consequence, was just in that reckless state of mind, when he would have hesitated at no deed, however heinous. From a jovial, good-natured Indian, in the company of the Hibernian, he was transformed into a sullen, vindictive savage in the presence of the gentle wife of Harvey Richter. He supported himself against the door and seemed undecided whether to enter or not. The alarm of Cora Richter was so excessive that she endeavored to conceal it.

"What do you wish?" she asked.

Edward S. Ellis

"Where Misser Richter?"

"Gone to the village," she replied, bravely resolving that no lie should cross her lips if her life depended upon it.

"When come back?"

"In an hour or so perhaps."

"Where Ted?"

"He has gone hunting."

"Big lie—he drunk—don't know nothing—lay sleep on ground."

"How do you know? Did you see him?"

"Me gib him fire-water—much like it—drink good deal—tumble over like tree hain't got root."

"Did you ever give it him before?" asked the young wife, her curiosity supplanting her alarm for the moment.

"Gib him offin—gib him every day—much like it—drink much."

Again the wife's instinctive fear came back to her, and she endeavored to conceal it by a calm, unimpassioned exterior.

"Won't you come in and rest yourself until Mr. Richter returns?"

"Don't want to see him," replied the savage, sullenly.

"Who do you wish to see then?"

"You—t'ink much of you."

The wife felt as if she would sink to the floor. There was something in the tones of his voice that had alarmed her from the first. She was almost certain this savage intended rudeness, now that he knew the missionary himself was gone. She glanced up at the rifle which was hung above the fireplace. It was charged, and she had learned how to fire it since her marriage. Several times she was on the point of springing up and seizing it and placing herself upon the defensive. Her heart throbbed wildly at the thought, but she finally concluded to resort to such an act only at the last moment. She might still conciliate the Indian by kindness, and after all, perhaps he meditated no harm or rudeness.

"Come and sit down then, and talk with me awhile," said she, as pleasantly as it was possible.

The savage stumbled forward a few feet, and dropped into a seat, where he glared fully a minute straight into the face of the woman. This was the most trying ordeal of all, especially when she raised her own blue eyes, and addressed him. It seemed impossible to combat the fierce light of those orbs, although she bore their scrutiny like a heroine. He had seated himself near the door, but he was close enough for her to detect the fumes of the liquor he had drank, and she knew a savage was never so dangerous as when in a half-intoxicated condition.

"Have you come a long distance?" she asked.

"Good ways—live up north."

"You are not a Sioux, then?"

"No—don't like Sioux—bad people."

"Why do you come in their neighborhood—in their country?"

"'Cause I want to—*come see you.*"

"You must come again—"

At this juncture, the child in the cradle awoke and began crying. The face of the savage assumed an expression of ferocity, and he said, abruptly:

"Stop noise—me tomahawk if don't."

As he spoke he laid his hand in a threatening manner upon his tomahawk, and the mother sprung up and lifted the infant in her arms for the purpose of pacifying it. The dreadful threat had almost unnerved her, for she believed the savage would carry it out upon the slightest pretext. But before that tomahawk should reach her child, the mother must be stricken to the earth. She pressed it convulsively to her breast, and it quickly ceased its cries. She waited until it closed its eyes in slumber and then some impulse prompted her to lay it upon the bed, and to place herself between it and the Indian, so that she might be unimpeded in her movements if the savage should attempt harm to her or her offspring.

Several moments now passed without the Indian speaking. The interval was occupied by him in looking around the room and examining every portion upon which it was possible to rest his gaze. The survey completed, he once more fixed his scrutiny upon the young wife, and suddenly spoke in his sententious, abrupt manner.

"Want sunkin eat."

This question was a relief, for it afforded the wife an opportunity of expressing her kindness; but, at the same time, it caused a more rapid beating of her heart, since to procure what was asked, she would be compelled to pass out of the door, and thus not only approach him much more closely than she was willing, but it would be necessary to leave him alone with her infant until her return.

She was in a painful dilemma, to decide whether it was best to refuse the visitor's request altogether or to comply with it, trusting to Providence to protect them both. A casual glance at the Indian convinced her that it would be dangerous to thwart his wishes longer; and, with an inward prayer to God, she arose and approached the door. As she passed near him, he moved and she involuntarily quickened her step, until she was outside. The Indian did not follow, and she hurried on her errand.

She had gone scarcely a yard, when she heard him walking across the floor, and detected at the same moment, the cry of her infant. Fairly beside herself with terror, she ran back in the house, and saw the savage taking down her husband's rifle. The revulsion of her feelings brought tears to her eyes, and she said:

"I wish you would go away, I don't like you."

"Kiss me—den I go!" said he, stepping toward her.

"Keep away! keep away!" she screamed, retreating to the door and yet fearing to go out.

"Kiss me—tomahawk pappoose!" said the savage, placing his hand upon the weapon.

The young wife placed her hands over her face and sobbed

　　　　　　Edward S. Ellis

aloud. She did not hear the cat-like footsteps of the savage, as he approached. His long arm was already stretched forth to clasp her, when the door was darkened, a form leaped into the room, and with the quickness of lightning, dealt the savage a tremendous blow that stretched him limp and lifeless upon the floor.

"Move a limb and I will kill you!" shouted the young missionary, his face all ablaze with passion. "Cora, has he harmed you?"

"No, no, no, Harvey; have you not already killed him?"

"Pity that I haven't. He is not fit to live."

"Dear Harvey, you are carried away by your passion. Do restrain yourself."

Woman-like, the only emotion of Cora Richter was that of commiseration for the poor wretch that had been stricken down by the hand of her husband. She saw the blood trickling from his face and knew that he was dreadfully injured. The missionary, too, began to become more calm and collected; and yet, while regretting the occasion, he could but think he had done his simple duty to his insulted wife. Had he been prepared as he entered the door, he would have shot the savage dead in his tracks.

Harvey picked up his rifle that lay in the middle of the floor, and approached the prostrate Indian. After pushing and shaking, he gave signs of returning consciousness, and at length arose to his feet. His nose had bled copiously, and one eye was "closed," as if he had been under the manipulation of some pugilist.

The wife brought a basin of water, and offered a bandage,

while Harvey proffered his assistance. But the Indian, without speaking, motioned them aside, and made his way out the door. On the threshold he paused a moment and looked back—and that look Harvey Richter will remember to his dying day.

Both breathed freer when he had gone. They then looked in each other's faces a moment and the wife sunk into her husband's arms.

"Did I not do right, Cora?"

"Yes; oh, yes; but, Harvey, this will not be the last of it. You have made an enemy of that Indian, and he can never be made a friend."

"Such is often the result of doing your simple duty. Let us therefore trust to God and say no more about it. Ah! here comes Teddy."

The Irishman at this moment entered the door. He was still under the influence of liquor though he made ludicrous efforts to conceal it. The wife found opportunity to communicate to her husband all that had been told her, before the conversation had progressed far. The peril which she had so narrowly escaped decided the missionary to be severely just with his servant.

"Teddy, where have you been?"

"Won't that spake for itself?" he replied, holding up a handsome string of fish. "Begorrah, but it was mighty poor luck I had hunting."

"I should judge you had discovered something unusual from your strange actions."

The face of the Irishman flushed scarlet, and his confusion was distressing. "Teddy," he continued, "I am displeased at the manner in which you have acted for the last week or two. Had it not happened that I left the village sooner than usual to-day, most probably my wife and son would have been killed."

The fellow was completely sobered.

"What is it ye say, Mister Harvey?"

"For several days you have failed to return in the time you promised, so that I have been compelled to leave them alone and unprotected. This afternoon, an Indian came in the house and threatened the life of both my wife and child—"

"Where the divil is he?" demanded Teddy, springing up; "I'll brake ivery bone in his body."

"He is gone, never to return I trust."

"Be the powers! if I could but maat him—"

"Do not add falsehood to your conduct. He said that you and he have met constantly and drank liquor together."

The expression of blank amazement was so genuine and laughable that the missionary could hardly repress a smile. He felt that his last remark was hardly fair. Teddy finally burst out.

"'Twas that owld Mahogany copperskin; but did I iver 'xpact he was up to *sich* a trick and he would niver have l'aved me a-fishing. Oorah, oorah!" he muttered, gnashing his teeth together. "What a miserable fool I *have* been. He to come here and insult me mistress after professin' the kindest regards. May I be made to eat rat-tail files for potaties if iver I trust red-skin honor again!"

"It strikes me that you and this precious savage had become quite intimate. I suppose in a few weeks longer you would have left us and lived with him altogether."

The tears trickled down Teddy's cheeks, and he made answer in a meek, mournful tone:

"Plaise forgive me, Mister Harvey, and Miss Cora. Yees both knows I would die for yees, and it was little I dr'amed of a savage iver disecrating this house by an ungentlemanly act. Teddy never'll sarve yees the like agin."

"I have no faith in the promises of a man who is intemperate."

The Irishman raised his hand to heaven:

"May the good Father above strike me dead if I iver swallow another drop! Do yees belave me now. Mister Harvey?"

"You must not place the reliance in your own power, Teddy. Ask His assistance and you'll succeed."

"I'll do so; but, ye saa, the only mill where I could get the cursed stuff was of this same Indian, and as I politely towld him I'd practice wid me gun on him if he offered me anither drop, and, as I'd pick him off now, after this shine, as quick as I would a sarpent, it ain't likely he'll bother me agin."

"I hope not, but I have the same apprehension as Cora that he will return when we least expect him. We must manage so that we are never both away from the house at the same time. It is now getting well along in the afternoon, Teddy; you may prepare your fish for supper."

The Irishman obediently moved away, and the young missionary and his wife were left together.

CHAPTER V

GONE!

Alas, alas, fair Inez, She went away with song, In sounds that sang Farewell, Farewell To her you've loved so long.

—HOOD

Alertness or watchfulness is sure to succeed the accomplishment of an enemy's designs. The moment danger is over, then the most vigilant preparations against it are made. The burglar knows better than to visit the same house two nights in succession. He is wise enough to wait until time has lulled the inmates into fancied security.

With such an interest at stake as had Harvey Richter, one may well believe that no precaution was neglected which could operate to defeat the designs of the savage whom he had driven in anger from his door. He changed his hour of visitation from the afternoon to the forenoon. Teddy needed no admonition against leaving the house during his absence. He kept watch and ward over the house as if he would atone by vigilance for past shortcomings.

The missionary had dwelt long enough among the Indians to

Edward S. Ellis

gain a pretty accurate estimate of their character. What troubled him most, therefore, was a conviction that the savage's revenge, though delayed for ten years, for want of the convenient opportunity, was sure to be accomplished. He might have gone immediately to the north or east, there to remain with his own tribe until convinced that the moment had come to strike the blow—a blow, which no human influence, no personal danger, no suffering, could persuade him from inflicting upon the offending white man.

But there was no certainty even of delay. Did the savage believe the moment to strike propitious, he would be ready for the trial. Even then, he might be skulking in the woods, with his black eyes fixed upon the cabin. It will be perceived, that, did he contemplate the death of either of the parties concerned, he could have compassed it without difficulty. Opportunities offered every day for the fatal bullet to reach its mark; but the *insult* to the Indian was so great, that he contemplated a far sweeter compensation than death itself. Whatever that might be, time would be sure to develop it, and that, too, at the moment when least expected.

This fear became so ever-present and troublesome, that the missionary made it known in the village, where he could command the services of half a hundred warriors. A dozen at once made search through the woods to ascertain whether the savage was concealed anywhere in the vicinity. One of these chanced upon a trail, which, after following some distance, was lost in the river. This, however, he pronounced to be the trail of a *white man*. The suspected Indian evidently, had fled, and no trace was discovered of him.

Another source of annoyance was opened to Harvey. Since the shot at Teddy, nothing had occurred to remind them of the existence of the strange hunter, whose mysterious warnings had accompanied their advent into the country.

Richter could not believe that the man had left altogether, but regarded his actions with considerable equanimity, as it was apparent that his warning shots were intended rather to frighten than to kill. Harvey never would converse with his wife about this white foe, and had cautioned Teddy not to allude to him in her presence. The missionary had a strong hope that, some day, he would be brought face to face with this stranger, when an explanation would be secured and the annoyance ended. He therefore repeated his warning to the Irishman not to shoot the hunter, unless compelled to do so to save his own life; but rather to use every effort to secure him and bring him to the cabin.

About a week after the occurrence narrated, Teddy went fishing, leaving the husband and wife together. He followed the shore of the river about a half-mile downward, when he settled himself by a huge rock that projected a few feet into the water. He had just thrown his line into the stream, when he heard the crackling of bushes behind him, and, turning, saw the hunter walking in a direction parallel with the river, with his head bent, as if in thought. Apparently he was unsuspicious of the presence of any one.

Teddy at once sunk down to screen himself as he watched the movements of his old foe, out of all manner of patience with himself that he had left his rifle at home, and possessed only the arms that nature had furnished him. Still, he resolved that the man should be secured, if possible.

"Arrah, now, be aisy!" he whispered, "and yees may cotch a fish that didn't nibble at yer bait. Whisht! but do ye *saa* him? But *isn't* he a strappin' fellow, to be sure—a raal shark ten foot long, with claws like an alligator!"

The hunter walked but a few rods, when he seated himself upon a fallen tree, with his back toward the Irishman. This was the coveted opportunity.

"Yees have got the fellow now, Teddy, barring yees haven't got him at all, but that ain't saying ye won't get him. Be aisy now, and don't get excited! Jist be as wise as a rat and as still as a mouse, and ye'll catch the catamount, if he don't catch you, that is."

These self-admonitions were much needed, for the fellow was all tremulous with excitement and scarcely able to restrain himself. Waiting a few moments until he could tone down his nerves, he commenced making his way toward his victim. He exercised extreme caution until within a rod, when a twig snapped under his foot. He made ready to spring, for he was certain of being discovered; but, to his surprise, the hunter made no motion at all. He evidently was so absorbed in some matter as to be unconscious of what was passing around.

Slowly and stealthily Teddy glided toward the man, until he arose almost to the standing position, not more than a foot distant. Then slowly spreading out his arms, so as to inclose the form of the stalwart woodsman, he brought them together like a vise, giving utterance at the same time to an exultant "whoop."

"Yer days of thramping *this* country, and alarming paceable inhabitants are done wid, Mister Anaconda. So jist kaal over gracefully, say tin Ave Marias, and consider yourself in the hands of Gabriel sint for judgment."

All this time Teddy had been straining and hugging at the hunter as if determined to crush him, while he, in turn, had taken it very coolly, and now spoke in his gruff bass voice:

"Let go!"

"Let go! Well now, that's impudint, ye varlet. As if Teddy McFadden would let go hook and line, bob and sinker, whin he had got hold of a sturgeon. Be aisy now; I'll squaze the gizzard and liver iv ye togither, if ye doesn't yield gracefully."

"Let go, I say! Do you hear?".

"Yis, I hears, and that is the extint—"

Teddy's next sensation was as if a thunderbolt had burst beneath his feet, for he was hurled headlong full half a rod over the head of the hunter. Though considerably bruised, he was not stunned by the fall, and quickly recovered. Scratching his head, he cried:

"Begorrah, but yees can't repate *that* trick!" making a rush toward his antagonist, who stood calmly awaiting his onset.

"By heavens, I'll give you something different then!" said the man, as he caught him bodily in his arms, and running to the edge of the river, flung him sprawling into it. The water was deep, and it required considerable struggling to reach the shore.

This last prodigious exhibition of strength inspired the Irishman with a sort of respect for the stranger. Teddy had found very few men, even among frontiersmen and Indians, who could compete with him in a hand-to-hand struggle; yet, there was now no question but what he was overmatched, and he could but admire, in a degree, the man who so easily handled his assailant. It was useless to attack the enemy after such a repulse; so he quietly seated himself upon the shore.

"Would ye have the kindness, ye assassinating disciple of the crowner's jury, whin yees have jist shown how nately ye can dishpose of a man like meself, to tell me why it was you run so mighty harrd whin I took once before after yees? Why didn't ye pause, and sarve me then jist as ye have done? I'd jist like to know that before we go any further wid *this* matter."

"It wasn't because I feared you!" said the hunter, turning sullenly away, and walking into the wood.

"Farewell!" called out Teddy, waving his hand toward him. "Ye're a beauty, and yees have quite taking ways wid ye; but it wouldn't be safe for me to find yees lurking about the cabin, if I had a rifle in me hand. You'd have trouble to fling a bullet off as ye flung me. Be jabers, but *wasn't* that a nate thing, to be sure. I'll bet a thousand pounds which I niver had, that that fellow could draw the Mississippi up-stream if he was fairly hitched on to it. Ah, Teddy, you ain't much, afther all," he added, looking dolefully at his wet garments.

Teddy had been so completely outwitted that he was unwilling any one should know it. So he resolved to continue fishing until his clothes were thoroughly dry, and until he had secured enough fish to repay him for his journey. It was near the middle of the afternoon, and, as he had remained at home until the return of the young missionary from the village, there was nothing to disturb his labor, or sport as it might be called, except darkness itself.

During this same afternoon, Harvey Richter and his wife were sitting on a bench in front of their cabin. The day was warm, but, as the bench always was shaded, it was the ordinary resort of the young couple when the weather was sultry. The missionary had been reading, but the volume was laid aside, and he was smilingly watching his wife as she sported with the boy in her lap. The little fellow was in exuberant spirits, and the parents, as a matter of course, were delighted. Finally he betrayed signs of weariness, and in a few moments was asleep in his mother's arms.

"I think it was a wise thing, for several reasons—that of changing your hour from the afternoon to the forenoon," said the wife.

"Why do you think so?"

"We all feel more wearied and less inclination at this time of day for work than we do during the earlier hours. We could then be little together, but now nothing interferes with our afternoon's enjoyment of one another's society."

"That is true; but you see the Indians are more likely to be off fishing or hunting during the earlier part of the day. They have willingly conformed, however, to the change."

"I think it is more in accordance with your own disposition," smiled the wife, "is it not?"

"Yes; I am free to admit that my lazy body inclines to quiet and rest after partaking of a hearty dinner, as I have done to-day."

"If we think of rest at this early stage in our lives, how will it be when we become thirty or forty years older?"

"I refer only to the temporary rest of the body and mind, such as they must have after periods of labor and excitement. Such rest the youngest as well as the oldest requires. Be careful, Cora, you don't drop the little fellow!"

"Never fear," laughed the mother, as the youngster woke and commenced several juvenile antics more interesting to the parents than to any one else:

"How lively!" remarked the proud father. "It seems to me I never saw a child at his age as bright and animated."

And what father does not hold precisely the same opinion of his young hopeful?

"Look!" exclaimed the mother, "some one must be coming to see you."

An Indian woman was discernible among the trees, walking along the path at a rapid walk, as if she were greatly hurried. Her head was bent, but now and then she raised it and glanced toward the cabin, showing that that was her destination.

Passing from the shadow of the wood into the Clearing, the missionary recognized one of the worst women of the tribe. She had scoffed at his preaching, had openly insulted him, and during the first month or two had manifested a disposition approaching violence. To this Richter only answered by kindness; he used every means to conciliate her good-will, but thus far with indifferent success. Her husband, The-au-o-too, a warrior favorably inclined toward the white man, was thoughtful and attentive; and the good minister wondered that the savage did not restrain these unwomanly demonstrations upon his squaw's part.

She approached with rapid step, until she stood directly in front of them. Harvey saw that her countenance was agitated.

"Well, At-to-uck," said he, kindly, "you seem troubled. Is there anything I can do for you?"

"Me ain't trouble," she answered, using English as well as her very imperfect knowledge would admit. "Me ain't trouble —*me* ain't."

"Who may it be then?"

"The-au-o-too—he *much* trouble. Sick—in woods—die—*berry* sick."

"What do you mean, At-to-uck?" asked the missionary, his interest strongly awakened. "Has anything befallen your husband?"

"He fall," she answered, eagerly, catching at the helping word, "he fall—much hurt—die—die—won't got well."

"Where is he?"

She spun around on one foot, and pointed deeper into the woods. "He dere—lay on back—soon die."

"And he wishes me to see him; is that it?"

She nodded her head vigorously, but made no answer for a moment. Then she suddenly broke forth:

"Send At-to-uck to git good man—hurry—berry hurry—he die—won't live. The-au-o-too say hurry—die soon—won't see good man—Riher."

Harvey looked at his wife. "What must I do, Cora? It will not do to leave you, as Teddy may not return for several hours, and yet this poor Indian should be attended in his dying moments."

"You should go, Harvey; I will not fear."

He turned to the squaw in perplexity.

"How far away is The-au-o-too?"

"Not much far—soon find—most dead."

"It may be," he said in a low tone, "that he can be got to the house, although it would be no easy matter for us two to bring him."

"I think your duty calls you to the dying man."

"I ought to be there, but I tell you, Cora, I don't like this leaving you alone," said he, impressively. "You know we made up our minds that it should never occur again."

"There must be occasions when it cannot be avoided, and this is one of them. By refusing to attend this man, you may not only neglect a great duty, but incur the ill-will of the whole tribe. You know the disposition of this woman."

The latter, at this point, began to give evidence of agitation, and to remark in her broken accents that The-au-o-too was dying and would be dead before they could reach him. The missionary, in sore perplexity, looked at his wife.

"Go," she said, or rather signified without speaking.

"I will," he said, rising with an air of decision. "God grant I may never regret this."

"I trust you never will."

He kissed the infant, embraced his wife and then signified to the squaw to lead the way.

"Keep up a good heart," he added, turning, as he moved away.

The wife smilingly nodded her head but said nothing. It did

not escape the notice of her husband that there were tears in her eyes, and he half resolved to remain with her after all, but the next moment he moved on.

The squaw took the well-beaten track, walking very rapidly and often looking back to see that she was followed. Her strangeness of manner the missionary attributed to her excitement regarding her husband. Several times she exhibited hesitation, and once or twice muttered something that was unintelligible to him.

When they were about half-way to the village, she paused.

"Well, At-to-uck, what is the matter now?"

"Mebbe dead."

"Oh, I hope not," he answered, cheerfully. "Do you turn off here?"

She answered in the affirmative and asked him to lead the way.

"No; I am unacquainted, and you ought certainly to know where to find your dying husband better than I do."

She took the duty of guide upon herself again, and advanced but a rod, when she abruptly paused. "Hark! hear groan? Me hear him."

Harvey listened intently but heard nothing. Knowing that the hearing of the Indians is marvelously acute, he believed the squaw had heard sounds of distress; but, instead of quickening her steps, she now moved more slowly than ever.

"Have you lost your way, At-to-uck?"

Edward S. Ellis

"No," she answered, in a significant voice.

The suspicions of the missionary that had been slumbering were now fully roused.

"What do you mean then?"

The squaw turned full around and gave a leer which, if possible, made her face more hideous than ever. Without thinking Harvey caught her by the arm and shook her sharply.

"Explain this, At-to-uck. What is the meaning of this?"

"He-he-e-e-e! *big* fool. The-au-o-too hunt—*no hurt*!"

A sharp reproof arose to the missionary's lips, but deeming it would be lost upon such a person, he merely turned his back upon her and walked away. She called and taunted him, but he was the last man who could have been roused to anger by such means, and he walked, with his arms folded, slowly and deliberately away toward the path.

It had not occurred, as yet, to the mind of Richter that anything more than a simple annoyance to himself was contemplated by this proceeding; but, as he resumed his steps homeward, a suspicion flashed upon him which almost checked the beating of his heart. "God save it being so!" was his mental prayer, as he hurried forward. A moment later he was on a full run.

The afternoon was well advanced, but he soon caught a glimpse of his cabin through the trees. Before this, however, he had detected the outcries of his infant, which struck him as a favorable omen, and he abated his speed somewhat. But, as he came into the Clearing, his heart gave a great bound, as he saw his child lying upon the ground some distance from the house. His anxiety was so distressing that he dashed by it into the cabin.

"Cora, Cora, what is the matter? Where have you concealed yourself? Why this untimely pleasantry?"

He came out again, caught up the infant and attempted to soothe it, all the time looking wildly about in the hope of seeing the returning mother.

"CORA! CORA!" he again called in agonized tones, but the woods gave back only the hollow echo. For a few moments he was fairly beside himself; but, at the end of that time, he began to reason more calmly. He attempted to persuade himself that she might return, but it was useless; and with a sort of resigned despair, he looked about him for signs of the manner in which she was taken away.

The most convincing evidence was not wanting. The ground was trampled and torn, as if there had been a violent struggle; and, inexperienced as were his eyes, he detected the unmistakable impress of a moccasin upon the soft earth, and in the grass. The settle, too, was overturned and the baby lay in the grass as if tossed there by the act of some other arm, than a mother's.

CHAPTER VI

THE LOST TRAIL

"'Twas night—the skies were cloudless blue,
And all around was hushed and still,
Save paddle of the light canoe,
And wailing of the whippowill."

On that sunny afternoon, the fish in a particular locality of a tributary of the Mississippi did not take the bait very well. The spot to which we refer was that immediately surrounding Teddy, whose patience was well-nigh exhausted. There he sat for several tedious hours, but had secured only two nibbles at his line, neither of which proved to be anything more.

"Begorrah, but it must be they'se frightened by meself, when that ould scalliwag give me a fling into the stream. Jabers! *wasn't* it done nately. Hallo! there's a bite, not bigger, to be sure, than a lady's fut, but a bull-pout it is I know."

He instantly arose to his feet, as if he were about to spring in the water, and stood leaning over and scanning the point where his line disappeared in the stream, with an intense interest which the professional angler alone can appreciate.

But this, like all others, proved a disappointment, and he soon settled down into his waiting but necessary attitude of rest.

"A half-hour more of sunshine, and then these same pants will be the same as if they've niver saan water, barring it's mighty seldom they have or they wouldn't be in this dirty condition. Arrah! what can be the m'aning of that?"

Faintly but distinctly through the long stretch of woods came the sound of his name. It was repeated again and again until the Irishman was convinced beyond all possibility of mistake.

"What is up now?" he asked of himself as he drew in his line. "That is Mister Harvey's voice sure, and he is calling as though he was in a mighty hurry. Faith, and I must not linger! If anything *should* happen whin I was away I'd feel wus'n old Boney at Watherloo whin he lost the day an' his crown."

The line was soon stowed away, and Teddy made his way at a half-walk and ran in a homeward direction. He had gone about a hundred rods when he paused and listened. Clearer and more distinctly came his name in tones whose earnest entreaty could not be mistaken. Teddy rose on his heels and made reply to the hail, to assure his master, if possible, that he was approaching with all speed.

The Irishman's words were yet lingering in his mouth, when another and more terrible sound reached his ears. It was that of a suppressed, half-smothered woman's scream—a sort of gasp of terror. It was so short and so far away that it was impossible to tell its direction. He stopped, his heart beating like a hammer, but he heard no more.

Edward S. Ellis

"God protect me, but there's something gone wrong at the cabin!" he exclaimed, dashing forward through the wood at a reckless rate. A few moments later it came in view, and he then saw his master walking to and fro, in front of the house, with the child in his arms. His manner and deathly pale face confirmed the forebodings of Teddy's heart.

"What's the matter, Mister Harvey? What's the matter?"

"*That Indian has carried Cora away!*" was the agonized reply.

"Where has the owld divil carried her?" very naturally asked the Hibernian.

"I do not know! I do not know! but she has gone, and I fear we shall never see her again alive."

"May me owld head be scraped wid a scalping-knife, an' me hands be made into furnace-grates for being away," ejaculated the servant, as the tears streamed down his cheeks.

"No, Teddy, you are not in the least to blame, nor is it my fault," impetuously interrupted the missionary.

"Till me how it was, Mister Harvey."

The husband again became composed and related what is already familiar to the reader. At its close, Teddy dashed into the house and brought out his rifle.

"I'll murther that At-to-uck, be me sowl, and then I'll murther that haythen assassinator, an' iverybody that gits in me way. Be the powers of the saints and divils, but I'll murther somebody. May the divil roast me if I—"

"Hold!" said the missionary, who by this time was himself again. "The first thing to be attended to is pursuit. We must not lose a second. We can never follow them ourselves through the wood. Hold the child, while I go to the village and get some of the Indians to help us."

Teddy took the child that had cried itself asleep, and the missionary started on a full run up the river. When he reached the settlement, it required but a moment to make his errand known. A dozen warriors volunteered at once, for these dozen would have laid down their lives for their faithful instructor. Many of the squaws also gave utterance to dismal howls upon learning what had befallen their pale-faced sister. Had the missionary chosen to tell the part taken by At-to-uck in the affair, it may be reasonably doubted whether her life would have been spared. But he was not the man to do such a thing. Knowing how anxious Teddy would be to participate in the pursuit, he secured the wife of one of the Christian Indians to return with him, and take charge of the boy during their absence.

At the time of the missionary's visit, the chief and his principal warriors were absent on an expedition to the north. Although holding little interest himself in the mission of the minister among his people, he would undoubtedly have led a party to the search for the audacious savage who had abducted the respected white woman; and, had he been overtaken, a swift and merciless retribution would have fallen upon the trangressor's head.

Harvey Richter deemed it best to take but a few Indians with him. Accordingly he selected five that he knew to be skillful, and with them hurried at once in the direction of his cabin. He saw with a sinking heart, as he returned, that the sun was already low in the horizon, and the woods were becoming dark and gloomy. Teddy was at his post chafing like a confined lion.

"This woman, Teddy, will take care of the boy, so that you may join us in the search."

"Bliss you for that! It would be the hardest work of me life to stay here when I thought there's a chance of gitting a whack at that thaiving villian. Oh, *if* I could only git howld of him, I wouldn't l'ave a piece of him big enough to spit on."

"I think there's little probability of either of us obtaining a glimpse of him. We must rely upon these Indians to take the trail and follow it to the end."

"They're like the hounds in the owld country, barring they go on two legs an' don't stick their noses in the ground, nor howl whin they git on trail. They're mighty handy to have around ye at such a time as this, if they be savages wid only a spark of Christianity in 'em not bigger than a tobaccy pipe."

"It will be impossible, I think, for the savage to conceal traces of his flight, and, if there be any chance of coming up with him, these men will surely do so."

"But suppose Miss Cora should be tomahawked and—"

"Don't mention it," said the missionary, with a shudder.

While these words were interchanged, the Indians had employed the time more profitably in solving the meaning of the footsteps upon the ground. A slight whoop announced the trail's discovery, and when the missionary turned, he saw the whole five gliding off in a line through the woods. They went in "Indian file," and resembled a huge serpent making its way with all swiftness toward its prey.

Our two friends started at once after them. On reaching the edge of the Clearing Teddy asked, abruptly:

"If the haythen comes back to the cabin while we's be gone?"

"Impossible! he cannot."

"Spowsen he hides his track in that manner, he may take a notion to gobble up the little boy."

"He would not dare—"

Nevertheless, the remark of his servant alarmed the missionary, and he hesitated. There might be foundation for what had been said. The savage finding the pursuit too close to escape with his prey, might slay her and then return stealthily to the cabin and dispatch the boy. It would not do to leave him alone with the Indian woman.

"I can afford little assistance in the hunt, and will remain behind. Hurry on, Teddy, or they will be too far away for you to follow."

The Hibernian shot off through the trees, at a rate that soon exhausted him, while Harvey Richter returned within his cabin, there to keep company with his great woe, until the return of the pursuers brought tidings of the lost one.

An Indian on the trail is not likely to permit any trivial cause to turn him aside, and the five Sioux made rapid progress so long as the light in the wood allowed them to do so. This, however, was a comparatively short time; and, after progressing fitfully and uncertainly for several hundred yards, they finally drew up to wait until the morrow.

The trail, instead of taking the direction of the river, as the pursuers believed it would, ran precisely parallel to it. So long as the savage kept away from the stream—that is, so long as he did not take to a canoe—his trail could be followed with absolute certainty, and he be overtaken beyond doubt. Impeded by an unwilling captive, he could not avoid a rapid gain upon him by his pursuers; and to escape certain capture, he must either abandon his prey or conceal his flight by resorting to the river.

It might be, and the pursuers themselves half believed, that the fleeing Indian did not fear a pursuit by any of his own race, in which case he could make a leisurely escape, as the unpracticed white men could not have followed him for a half-mile through the wilderness. If this were really the case, the Sioux were confident of coming up with him before the morrow's sun should go down.

The Indians had paused but a few moments, when a great tearing and scrambling was heard, and Teddy came panting upon them.

"What be yees waiting for?" he demanded. "Tired out?"

"Can't go furder—dark—wait till next day."

"I'm sorry that yees didn't stand it bitter. I can go some ways further meself if yees'll be kind enough to show me the trail. But, yees don't pant or blow a bit, so I can't think ye're too much tired."

"Too dark—can't see—wait till sun."

"Oh, begorrah! I didn't understand ye. The Injin 'l' git a good start on us, won't he though?"

"Ain't Injin—*white man*!"

"A white man, does ye say, that run off wid Miss Cora?"

Two of the Indians replied in the affirmative.

Teddy manifested the most unbounded amazement, and for a while, could say nothing. Then he leaped into the air, struck the sides of his shoes with his fingers, and broke forth:

"It was that owld hunter, may purgatory take him! Him and that owld Mahogany, what made me drunk—blast his sowl—have been hid around in the woods, waiting for a chance to do harm, and one is so much worse than t'other yees can't tell both from which. Och! if I but had him under the sight of me gun."

The spot upon which the Indians and Teddy were standing was but a short distance from the village, and yet, instead of returning to it, they started a small fire and lay down for the night. *They were upon the trail,* and nothing was to turn them aside from it until their work was completed, or it was utterly lost to them.

Teddy was more loth than they to turn his face backward, but, under the circumstances, he could not forget the sad, waiting husband at home. So he returned to the cabin, to make him acquainted with the result of their labors thus far.

"If the Indian only avoids the river, he may be overtaken, but if he takes to that, I am fearful he can never be found."

"Be me sowl, Mr. Harvey, but thim savages says he's not an Injin, but a *white man,* and yees know they cannot be mistook fur they've got eyes like hawks, and sinses sharper than me only needle, which, begorrah, hasn't got a point."

"Can it be that Bra—that that hunter has done me this great

wrong?" said the missionary, correcting himself so dextrously that his servant failed to observe it. "Has such been the revenge that he has been harboring up for so many years? And he has followed us these hundreds of miles for the purpose of striking the blow!"

"The owld haythen assassinator! The bloodthirsty beast, the sneakin' dog, the dirthy jail-bird, the—"

"He has not shot either of us when we were at his mercy, for the purpose of lulling us into security, the better to obtain his revenge, and oh, he has succeeded how well!"

The strong man, who still sat in the front of his cabin, where he might catch the first sound of returning footsteps, now covered his face, and his whole form heaved with emotion. Teddy began to feel uncomfortable. He arose, walked to and fro, and wiped the tears from his own cheeks. Despite his tears, however, he recognized in the exclamations of his master a reference to some mystery which he had long suspected, but which had never been cleared up. The missionary must have met this strange hunter before this encounter in the wilderness, and his identity, and the cause of his deadly enmity, must, also, be known. Teddy had a great curiosity; but, as his master had repulsed his inquiries upon a previous occasion, he forbore to make any reference to it. He walked backward and forward until the good man's emotion had subsided somewhat, and then he said:

"Good Master Harvey, the owld cabin is so lonely wid the form of Miss Cora gone, that it's meself that couldn't very well stay here till morning. So, wid yer leave jist, I'll return to the Injins, so as to be ready to folly the trail bright and early in the mornin'."

"And how do you suppose I feel, Teddy?"

"God save us! It can be no worse than meself."

"I am willing that you should go."

The missionary had need, indeed, for the sustaining power which can come only from above. The faithful Indian woman remained with his child through the night, while he, with bare head, and hands griped together, paced backward and forward until the morrow's sun had risen. How he prayed and agonized in spirit during those long, lonely hours, God and himself only know. When the day had fairly dawned, he entered the house, lay down wearily, and slept a "long and troubled sleep."

With a heavy heart Teddy made his way back through the woods to where the Indians were congregated. They were seated around the camp-fire engaged in smoking, but did not exchange nor utter a syllable. They all understood each other, and therefore there was no need of talk. The Irishman seated himself beside them, and joined an hour or two in smoking, when they all lay down and slumbered.

All with the exception of Teddy, who could not sleep. He rolled hither and thither, drew deep sighs, and took new positions, but it availed nothing. The events of the past day had driven sleep far from his eyelids, and he soon gave over the effort altogether. Rising to a sitting position, he scratched his head (which was significant only of abstraction of thought), and gazed meditatively into the smoldering embers.

While seated thus, an idea suddenly came to him which brought him instantly to his feet. The fact that it had not occurred to the Indians he attributed to their inferior shrewdness and sagacity. He recalled that the abduction of the young wife took place quite late in the afternoon; and, as she must be an unwilling captive of course, she would know

　　　　Edward S. Ellis

enough to hinder the progress of the man so as to afford her friends a chance to overtake them. Such being the case, the hunter would find himself compelled to encamp for the night, and therefore he could be but a short distance away. The more the Irishman reflected, the more he became convinced that his view was right; and, we may state, that for once, at least, his supposition had a foundation to stand upon.

The matter, as has been evident from the first to the reader, rested entirely upon the impossibility of following the trail at night. Thus far it had maintained its direction parallel with the river, and he deduced that it must continue to do so. Such being the case, the man could be reached as well during the darkness as daylight.

Teddy concluded not to awaken the savages, as they would hardly coincide with him. So he cautiously rose to his feet, and walking around them, made off in the darkness. He was prudent enough to obtain an idea of the general direction before starting, so as to prevent himself going astray; after which he pressed the pursuit with all possible speed. At intervals he paused and listened, but it seemed as if everything excepting himself was asleep. He heard no sound of animal or man: He kept his eyes flitting hither and thither, for he had hopes of chancing upon the camp-fire of the abductor.

It is always a difficult matter to keep one's "reckoning" in the woods. If they be of any extent, it requires extraordinary precautions upon the part of an inexperienced person to prevent himself from being lost. Should he endeavor to travel by night, it would be almost a miracle indeed if he could save himself from going totally astray.

Teddy had every disadvantage to contend against, and he had not journeyed a half-hour, when his idea of his own position was just the opposite of truth. As he had not yet become aware of it, however, it perhaps was just as well as if he had committed no error. He was pressing forward, with that peculiar impelling feeling that it was only necessary to do so ultimately to reach his destination, when a star-like glimmer caught his eye. Teddy stopped short, and his heart gave a great bound, for he believed the all-important opportunity had now come. He scanned the light narrowly, but it was only a flickering point, such as a lantern would give at a great distance at night. The light alone was visible, but no flame. It was impossible to form any correct idea of its location, although, from the fact that the nature of the wood must prevent the rays penetrating very far, he was pretty certain it was comparatively close at hand.

With this belief he commenced making his way toward it, his movements certifying his consciousness that a mis-step would prove fatal. To his dismay, however, he had advanced but a dozen steps or so when the light disappeared, and he found it impossible to recover it. He moved from side to side, forward and backward, but it availed nothing, and he was about to conclude it had been extinguished, when he retreated to his starting-point and detected it at once.

Keeping his eye fixed upon it, he now walked slowly, but at the same point as before it disappeared. This, he saw, must arise from some limb, or branch or tree interfering, and it only remained for him to continue advancing in the same line. Having proceeded a hundred rods or so, he began to wonder that he still failed to discover it. Thinking he might be mistaken in the distance, he went forward until he was sure he had passed far beyond it, when he turned and looked behind him. Nothing but the dim figures of the tree-trunks rewarded his gaze.

Fully a half-hour was spent in wandering to and fro in the

Edward S. Ellis

further efforts to locate the light that had caught his eye, and he finally sought to obtain his first stand-point. Whether he succeeded or not Teddy never could tell, but he never saw nor learned anything more regarding the camp-fire to which he was confident that he had been in such close proximity.

About this time, which was in the neighborhood of midnight, Teddy made the discovery that he was lost, and, like a sensible person, gave up all efforts to right himself. He was so wearied that he did not awake until daylight, when he was aroused by the five Indians, whose trail-hunt led them to the spot where he lay sleeping.

The trail was now followed rapidly for a half-mile when, as the pursuers had feared all along, it made a sudden bend to the river, upon the banks of which it was totally lost. Not to be baffled in this manner, a canoe was produced with which three crossed the river. The entire day was spent by these upon one bank, while the two other Indians and Teddy pursued the search for traces of the hunter's landing upon their own side of the stream. Not the slightest evidence was discovered that he had touched shore after embarking. The man had escaped, and even the eagle-eyed Sioux were compelled on the second night to return to their village with the sad announcement that the TRAIL WAS LOST!

CHAPTER VII

A HIBERNIAN'S SEARCH FOR THE TRAIL

"Oh I let me only breathe the air,   The blessed air that's breathed by thee; And, whether on its wings it bear Healing or death, 'tis sweet to me."

At the close of a windy, blustering day in 1821, two men were seated by a camp-fire in the depths of the wilderness of the northwest. The wind howled through the branches with a moaning sound such as often heralds the approach of bitter cold weather; and a few feathery flakes of snow that sailed along on the wind, proved that the season of storms was close at hand.

The fire was built down deep in a sort of gorge, where its cheery, crackling blaze could not be seen by any one until he was nearly upon it. The men sat with their pipes in their mouths, their rifles beside them and their feet toward the fire. From appearances they were on the best of terms. One of them needs no introduction, as he is our old friend Teddy, who evidently feels at home in his new situation. The other is a man of much the same build although somewhat older. His face, where it is not concealed by a heavy, grizzly beard, is covered by numerous scars, and the border of one eye is

Edward S. Ellis

disfigured from the same cause. His dress and accouterments betray the hunter and trapper.

"And so, Teddy, ye're sayin' it war a white man that took away the missionary's wife, and hain't been heard on since. Let me see, you said it war nigh onto three months ago, warn't it?"

"Three months, come day after to-morrow. Begorrah, but it's not I that'll forgit that same date to my dying day, if, indade, I forgit it at all, at all, even whin somebody else will be wearin' me clothes."

"It was a dirty trick, freeze me if it wasn't; but you can *allers* find a white man to do a mean trick, when you can't a copperskin; *that* you may set down as a p'inted fact, Teddy."

"I belaves ye, Mister Tim. An Indian is a poor mean thing at the bist, an' their squaws—kah! they are the dirtiest beasts that iver jabbered human lingo; an' their babies, I raaly belaves, is caught with a hook an' line in the muddy creeks where the catfish breed; but, fur all that, I don't think they could have been equal to this piece of wickedness. May the divil git howld of his soul. Blazes, but won't there be a big squeal in purgatory when the divil gits howld of him!" And Teddy seemed to contemplate the imaginary scene in Hades with a sense of intense satisfaction.

"But it's powerful strange you could never git on the trail. I don't boast of my own powers, but I'll lay if I'd been in the neighborhood, I'd 've found it and stuck to it like a bloodhound, till I'd 've throttled that thievin' wretch."

"The Sioux spent the bitter part of the day in the s'arch, an' meself an' siveral other savages has been looking iver since, and none of us have got so much as a scint of his shoe, bad luck to him."

"But, Teddy, what made him do it?" asked the trapper, turning his keen, searching eyes full upon him.

"There's where I can't answer yees."

"There be some men, I allow, so infarnal mean they'll do a mean thing just 'cause they *like* to do it, and it might be he's one of them."

"It's meself that belaves he howlds some spite agin Mister Harvey for something done in years agone, and has taken this means of revinging himself upon the good man, as I am sure niver did one of his fellow-creatures any harm."

"It may be there's been ill-blood a long time atween 'em, but the missionary couldn't a done nothin' to give the rapscallion cause to run off with his wife, 'less he'd run off with this hunter's old woman before, and the hunter was paying him for it."

"Git out wid yer nonsense!" said Teddy, impatiently. "It couldn't been a great deal, or if it was, it couldn't been done purposely, for I've growed up wid Mister Harvey, and knowed him ever since he was knee high to a duck, and he was *always* a boy that did more praying than fighting. The idea of *his* harming anyone, is *pre-pos-te-trous*. After the haythen had fired at us, the good man actilly made me promise not to do the wretch hurt if the chance was given me; and a mighty foolish thing, for all it was Master Harvey who towld me, fur I've had a chance or two at the spalpaan since. Oh blissed Virgin, why *didn't* I cut his wizzen for him whin I could have done it—that is, if I could!"

"And you've been huntin' 'im these three or four months

be you?"

"The same, yer honor, huntin' constantly, niver losing a day rain or shine, wid Indians an' widout 'em, cold, hungry and tired, but not a day of rist."

"Freeze me then, if you haven't got *grit*. Thar ain't many that would track through the woods that ar long. And ye haven't caught a glimpse of the gal nor heard nothin' of her?"

"Not a thing yet; but it's meself that 'xpacts to ivery day."

"In course, or ye wouldn' keep at the business. But s'pose, my friend, you go on this way for a year more—what then?"

"As long as I can thravel over the airth and Miss Cora isn't found, me faat shall niver find rest."

The trapper indulged in an incredulous smile.

"You'd be doing the same, Tim, if yees had iver laid eyes on Miss Cora or had iver heard her speak," said Teddy, as his eyes filled with tears. "God bliss her! she was worth a thousand such lives as mine—"

"Don't say nothin'" interrupted the trapper, endeavoring to conceal his agitation; "I've l'arned years ago what that business is. The copperskins robbed me of a prize I'll never git agin, long afore you'd ever seen one of the infarnal beings."

"Was she a swateheart?"

"Never mind—never mind; it'll do no good to speak of it now. She's *gone*—that's enough."

"How do you know she can't be got agin, whin—"

"She was tomahawked afore my eyes—ain't that enough?" demanded the trapper, indignantly.

"I axes pardon, but I was under the impression they had run away with her as they did with Miss Cora."

"Hang 'em, no! If they'd have done that I'd have chased 'em to the Pacific ocean and back agin afore I'd give 'em up."

"And that's what meself intends to do regarding Miss Cora."

"Yer see, yer don't know much about red-skins and their devilments, and therefore, it's my private opine, instead of getting the gal, they'll git you, and there'll be the end on't."

"Tim, couldn't yees make the s'arch wid me?" asked Teddy, in a deeply earnest voice. The trapper shook his head.

"Like to do't, but can't. It's time I was up to the beaver runs this night and had my traps set. Yer see I'm *compelled* to be in St. Louey at the end of six months and hain't got a day to spare."

"Mister Harvey has money, or, if he hasn't, he has friends in St. Louis, be the same token, that has abundance of it, and you'd find it paid you bitter in the ind than catching poor, innocent beavers, that niver did yees harm."

"I don't foller sich business for money, but I've agreed to be in St. Louey at the time I was tellin' you, and it's allers a p'int of honor with me to keep my agreements."

"Couldn't yees be doing that, and this same thing, too?"

Edward S. Ellis

"Can't do't. S'pose I should git on the trail that is lost, can yer tell me how fur I'd have to foller it? Yer see I've been in that business afore, and know what it is. Me and three others once chased a band of Blackfeet, that had carried off an old man, till we could see the peaks of the Rocky Mountains, and git a taste of the breath of wind that comes down from their ice and snow in middle summer."

"Didn't yees pursue the subjact any further?"

"We went fur enough to find that the nimble-footed dogs had got into the mountains, and that if we wanted to keep our ha'r, we'd only got to undertake to foller 'em thar. So we just tramped back agin, havin' our trouble for nothin'."

"Wasn't that about as poor a business, for yees, as this be for me, barring yees was hunting for an old man and I'm hunting for a young woman?"

"It warn't as foolish by a long shot, 'cause we *war on the trail* all the time, and kept it, while you've lost yours, and never'll be able to find it agin. We war so close more nor once that we reached their camp-fires afore the embers had died out and from the tops of two, three hills we got a glimpse on 'em on thar horses. We traveled all night a good many times, but it done no good as they done the same thing, and we found we war further away, if anything, next morning than we war at sundown. If we'd ever lost the trail so as not to find it we'd guv up and come home, but we never done that nor never lost more nor an hour in lookin' for it. You see," added the trapper, impressively, "you never have found the trail, and, therefore, there ain't the shadder of a chance."

"Begorrah, yees can't blame us whin we tried to the bist of our indeavor to find it and wasn't able."

"Yer done the best yer knowed, I s'pose; but why didn't four on 'em divide so as to let one go up one side the river and one t'other, and the same way down-stream. Yer don't s'pose that feller was able to keep paddlin' forever in the river, do yer? and jist so soon as he landed, jist so sure would one of them Sioux find the spot where he touched land, and foller him to his hole."

"Begorrah, if wees had only thought of that!"

"A Sioux is as cunning a red-skin as I ever found, and it's jist my opine every one of 'em *did* think of that same thing, but they didn't try it for fear they might catch the varmint! They knew their man, rest assured o' that."

Teddy looked up as if he did not comprehend the meaning of the last remark.

"'Cordin' to yer own showin', one of them infarnal copper-gals was at the bottom of the hull business, and it's like as not the men knowed about it, too, and didn't *want* to catch the gal!"

"There's where yees are mightily mistook, as Pat McGuire said whin his landlord called him honest, for ivery one of them same chocolate-colored gintlemen would have done their bist for Master Harvey. They would have cut that thaif's wizzen wid a mighty good will, I knows."

"Mebbe so, but I don't believe it!" said the hunter, with an incredulous shake of his head.

"Would ye have me give up the s'arch altogether?"

"Can't say that I would; howsumever, the chance is small, and ye'd better go west with me, and spend the winter in l'arning how to trap fur beaver and otter."

"What good might result from that?"

"None, as I knows on."

"Then it's meself that thanks yees for the offer and respectfully declines to accept the nomination. I'll jist elict meself to the office of sheriff an' go about these regions wid a s'arch-warrint in my shoes that'll niver let me rist until Miss Cora is found."

"Wal, I 'spose we'll part in the mornin' then. As yer say this are the first time you've got as fur north, I'll say I think you're nearer the trail than yer ever war yit."

"What might be the reason for that?" eagerly asked Teddy.

"I can't say what it is, only I kind o' feel it in my bones. Thar's a tribe of copperskins about a hundred miles to the north'ard, that I'll lay can tell yer *somethin'* about the gal."

"Indians? An' be what token would they be acquaint with her?"

"They're up near the Hudson Bay Territory line, and be a harmless kind of people. I stayed among 'em two winters and found 'em a harmless lot o' simpletons that wouldn't hurt a hair o' yer head. Thar's allers a lot of white people staying among 'em."

"I fails yit to see what they could be doing with Miss Cora."

"Mind I tells yer only what I *thinks*—not what I *knows*. It's my private opine, then, that that hunter has took the gal up among them Injins, and they're both living thar. If that be so, you needn't be afeard to go right among 'em, for the only thing yer'll have to look out fur will be the same old hunter himself."

This remark made a deep impression upon Teddy. He sat smoking his pipe, and gazing into the glowing embers, as if he could there trace out the devious, and thus far invisible, trail that had baffled him so long. It must be confessed that the search of the Hibernian thus far had been carried on in a manner that could hardly be expected to insure success. He had spent weeks in wandering through the woods, sleeping upon the ground or in the branches of some tree, fishing for awhile in some stream, or hunting for game—impelled onward all the time by his unconquerable resolve to find Cora Richter and return her to her husband. On the night that the five Sioux returned to the village, and announced their abandonment of the pursuit, Teddy told the missionary that he should never see him again, until he had gained some tidings of his beloved mistress, or had become assured that there could be no hope of her recovery. How long this peculiar means of hunting would have gone on, it is impossible to tell, but most probably until Teddy himself had perished, for there was not the shadow of a chance of his gaining any information of the lost one. His meeting with the trapper was purely accidental, and the hint thrown out by the latter was the reason of setting the fellow to work in the proper way.

The conversation was carried on for an hour or so longer, during which the trapper gave Teddy more advice, and told him the best manner of reaching the tribe to which he referred. He cautioned him especially against delaying his visit any longer, as the northern winter was almost upon them, and should he be locked in the wilderness by it, it would be almost impossible for him to survive its rigor; but if he should be among the tribe, he could rest in security and

Edward S. Ellis

comfort until the opening of spring. Teddy concluded to do as his companion advised, and, after more unimportant conversation, both stretched themselves out by the camp-fire and slept.

Just as the earliest light was breaking through the trees, the trapper was on his feet, rekindling the fire. Finding, after this was completed, that Teddy still slumbered, he brought him to his senses by several forcible applications of his foot.

"Begorrah, it's meself that's thinking yees 'av a mighty gintle way of coming upon one unawares, barring it's the same as a kick from a wild horse. I was dr'aming jist thin of a blast of powder in a stone quarry, which exploded under me feet, an' sint me up in the ship's rigging, an' there I hung by the eaves until a lovely girl pulled me in at the front door and shut it so hard that the chinking all fell out of the logs, and woke me out of me pleasint delusions."

The trapper stared at the Irishman incredulously, thinking him demented. Teddy's gaping and rubbing of his eyes with his fists, and, finally, his stretching of arms and legs, reassured Tim of the fellow's sanity, and he added:

"If yer hadn't woke just now, I'd tried ef lammin' yer over the head would've done any good."

"Yees might have done that, as long as ye plaised, fur me sconce got used to being cracked at the fairs in the owld country."

"I thought yer allers lived in this country."

"Not always, or how could I be an Irishman? God plaise I may niver live here long enough to forgit owld Ireland, the Gim of the Sea. What's the matter with yees now?"

The trapper having wandered a few yards from the camp-fire, had paused suddenly and stood gazing at the ground. Teddy was obliged to repeat his question.

"What is it yees have diskivered?"

"Sign, or ye may shoot me."

"Sign o' what?"

"Injins, ye wood-head! What else could I mean?"

Teddy now approached and narrowly examined the ground. His knowledge of wood-craft had been considerably increased during the past month or two, and he had no difficulty in distinguishing the imprint of a moccasin.

"Look at the infarnal thing!" exclaimed the trapper, in disgust. "Who'd a thort there'd 've been any of the warmints about, whin we took sich pains with our fire. Why the chap didn't send a piece of cold lead into each of our bread-baskets is more nor I can tell. It would've sarved us both right."

"P'raps thim tracks there was made fornenst the night, and that it's ourselves that was not here first."

"Don't yer s'pose I know all about *that*?" demanded the trapper, savagely. "Them tracks was made not more'n three or four hours ago."

As he spoke. Tim turned and followed it a rod or two, and then, as he came back, said:

"If I had the time I'd foller it; but it goes just t'other way from what I want to go. I think like 'nough it leads to the village that you want to find; so if yer'd like one of 'em to introduce yer to the rest on 'em, drive ahead and make his acquaintance. Maybe he kin tell yer something about the gal."

Teddy determined to follow the trail by all means. He partook of the morning meal with the trapper, exchanged a pleasant farewell, and then the two parted never to meet again.

The footprints were distinct and easily followed. Teddy advanced with long, loping strides, at a gait considerably more rapid than his usual one. He indulged in curious reveries as he followed it, fancying it to be an unfriendly Indian with whom a desperate collision must inevitably take place, or some friendly member of the tribe, of whom the trapper had told him, that would prove a boon companion to him. All at once he reached a small, marshy tract, where the trail was much more palpable; and it was here that he either saw or fancied the toes of the footprints turned *outward*, thus demonstrating that, instead of an Indian, he was following a white man.

The Hibernian's heart throbbed at the thought that he was upon the track of the strange hunter, with all probability of overtaking him. It caused his heart to throb violently to reflect how close he was upon the critical moment. Drawing a deep breath and closing his lips tightly, he pressed on ready for the conflict.

The trail continued as distinct as ever, and the pursuit suffered no interruption until it entered a deep swamp into which Teddy hesitated to enter, its appearance was so dark and forbidding. As he gazed into its gloomy depths, he was almost certain that he had discovered the *home* of the hunter. That at that moment the criminal was within its confines, where perhaps the beloved Cora was imprisoned, a miserable and pining captive. The thought maddened him, and he pressed forward so rashly that he soon found himself completely entrapped in a network of briers and brambles. Carefully withdrawing into the open wood, it suddenly occurred to him, that if the hunter had passed through the thicket, there was no earthly necessity of his doing it. He could pass around, and, if the footprints were seen upon the opposite side, it only remained to follow them, while, if they were not visible, it certified that he was still within the thicket and he could therefore shape his actions accordingly.

Teddy therefore made his way with patience and care around one end of the thicket. He found the distance more consider-able than he at first supposed. It was full an hour before he was fairly upon the opposite side. Here he made a careful search and was soon rewarded by finding unmistakable footprints, so that he considered it settled that the hunter had passed straight through the thicket.

"It's a quaar being he is entirely, when it's meself that could barely git into the thicket, and he might have saved his hide by making a short thramp around, rather than plunging through in this shtyle."

Teddy pressed on for two hours more, when he began to believe that he was close upon the hunter, who must have traveled without intermission to have eluded him thus far. He therefore maintained a strict watch, and advanced with more caution.

The woods began to thicken, and the Hibernian was brought to a stand-still by the sound of a rustling in the bushes. Proceeding some distance further, he came upon the edge of a bank or declivity, where he believed the strange hunter had laid down to rest. The footprints were visible upon the edge of the bank, and at the bottom of the latter was a mass of heavy undergrowth, so dense as effectually to preclude all observation of what might be concealed within it.

It was in the shrubbery, directly beneath him, that Teddy believed the hunter lay. He must be wearied and exhausted, and no doubt was in a deep sleep. Teddy was sure, in his enthusiasm, that he had obtained a glimpse of the hunter's clothes through the interstices of the leaves, so that he could determine precisely the spot where he lay, and even the position of his body—so eagerly did the faithful fellow's wishes keep in advance of his senses.

And now arose the all-important question as to what he should do. He might shoot him dead as he slept, and there is little question but what Teddy would have done it had he not been restrained by the simple question of expediency. The hunter was alone, and, if slain, all clue to the whereabouts of Mrs. Richter would be irrecoverably lost. What tidings that might ever be received regarding her, must come from the lips of him who had abducted her. If he could desperately wound the man, he might frighten him into a confession, but then Teddy feared instead of wounding him merely with his rifle, he would kill him altogether if he attempted to shoot.

After a full half-hour's deliberation, Teddy decided upon his course of action. It was to spring knife in hand directly upon the face of the hunter, pin him to the ground and then force the confession from his lips, under a threat of his life, the Irishman mercifully resolving to slay him at any rate, after he had obtained all that was possible from him.

Teddy did not forget his experience of a few months before when the hunter gave him an involuntary bath in the river. He therefore held his knife firmly in his right hand. Now that he had concluded what to do, he lost no time in carrying his plan into execution.

He took a crouching position, such as is assumed by the panther when about to spring upon its prey, and then drawing his breath, he leaped downward.

A yelping howl, an impetuous scratching and struggling of the furious mass that he attempted to inclose in his arms, told Teddy that instead of the hunter, he had pounced down upon an innocent, sleeping bear!

It was well for the Irishman that the bear was peaceably inclined, else his search for the lost trail might have terminated then and there. The brute, after freeing itself from its incubus, sprung off and made all haste into the woods, leaving Teddy gazing after it in stupefied amazement. He rose to his feet, stared at the spot where it had last appeared and then drew a deep sigh, and sadly shook his head.

"I say nothing! Be jabers! it's meself that can't do justice to the thame!"

Harvey Richter stood in his cabin-door, about five months after his great loss, gazing off toward the path which led to the Indian village, and which he had traveled so many, many times. Sad and weary was his countenance, as he stood, at the close of the day, looking into the forest, as if he expected that it would speak and reveal what it knew of his beloved partner, who was somewhere concealed within its gloomy depths. Ah, how many an hour had he looked, but in vain. The forest refused to give back the lost, nor did it breathe one word of her, to ease the gloom which hung so heavily upon his soul.

A footfall caught his ear, and turning, he saw Teddy standing before him. The face of the Irishman was as dejected as his own, and the widowed man knew there was scarce need of the question:

Edward S. Ellis

"Have you heard anything, Teddy?"

"Nothing, sir, saving that nothing is to be learnt."

"Not my will, but thine, oh God, be done!" exclaimed the missionary, reverently, and yet with a wailing sadness, that proved how unutterable was his woe.

CHAPTER VIII

THE TRAIL OF DEATH

These likelihoods confirm her flight from hence; Therefore, I pray you, stay not to discourse, But mount you presently.

—SHAKESPEARE

The trapper, after separating from the Irishman, pursued his way through the woods with a slow tread, as if he were deliberating some matter with himself. Occasionally he muttered and shook his head, in a manner that showed his conscience was getting the better of the debate, whatever it might be. Finally he paused.

"Yas, sir; it's a mean piece of business in me. 'Cause I want to cotch a few beavers I must let this gal be, when she has been lost to her husband already for three months. It's ongenerous, and *can't be done!*" he exclaimed, emphatically. "What if I does lose a few peltries when they're bringing such a good price down in St. Louey? Can't I afford to do it, when there's a gal in the matter?"

He resumed his walk as slowly and thoughtfully as before, muttering to himself.

Edward S. Ellis

"If I go, I goes alone; least I don't go with that Teddy, for he'd be sartin to lose my ha'r as sure as we got onto a trail. There's no calc'latin' the blunders of *such* a man. How he has saved his own scalp to this time is more nor I can tell, or himself neither, for that matter, I guess. I've been on many a trail-hunt alone, and if I goes—if I goes, why, *in course* I does!" he added, impetuously.

The resolution once taken seemed to afford him unusual pleasure, as it does with us all when the voice of conscience is a monitor that is heeded. He was tramping toward the west, and now that the matter was decided in his own mind, he paused again, as if he could better debate other matters that must in the circumstances necessarily present themselves.

"In the first place, there's no use of going any further on *this* track, for I ain't gettin' any nigher the gal, that's pretty sartin. From what that Teddy told me of his travels, it can't be that she's anywhere in these parts, for if she war, he couldn't have helped l'arning something of her in all this time. There's a tribe up north that I've heard was great on gettin' hold of white gals, and I think I'll make a s'arch in that direction afore I does anything else."

Nothing more remained for Tim but to carry out the resolution he had made, and it was characteristic of the man that he did it at once. Five minutes after the above words had been muttered, he was walking rapidly along in a northern direction, his rifle thrown over his arm, and a beaming expression of countenance that showed there were no regrets at the part he was acting. He had a habit of talking with himself, especially when some weighty or unusual matter obtruded itself. It is scarcely to be wondered, therefore, that he became quite talkative at the present time.

"I allers admire such adventur's as this, if they don't bring in anything more nor thanks. The style in which I've received them is allers worth more money nor I ever made trapping beavers. The time I cotched that little gal down on the Osage, that had been lost all summer, I thought her mother would eat me up afore she'd let me go. I believe I grinned all day and all night for a week after that, it made me think I was such a nice feller. Maybe it'll be the same way with this. Hello!"

The trapper paused abruptly, for on the ground before him he saw the unmistakable imprint of a moccasin. A single glance of his experienced eye assured him upon that point.

"That there are Injins in these parts is a settled p'int with me, and that red and white blood don't agree is another p'int that is settled. That track wasn't made there more nor two hours ago, and it's pretty sartin the one that made it ain't fur away at this time. It happens it leads to the north'ard, and it'll be a little divarsion to foller it, minding at the same time that there's an Injin in it."

For the present the trapper was on a trail, and he kept it with the skill and certainty of a hound. Over the dry leaves, the pebbly earth, the fresh grass, the swampy hollow—everywhere, he followed it with unerring skill.

"That Injin has been on a hunt," he muttered, "and is going back home agin. If it keeps in this direction much longer, I'll believe he's from the very village I'm hunting after. Heigh! there's something else up!"

He suddenly checked himself and began snuffing the air, as though it was tainted with something suspicious.

"I hope I may be shot if there ain't a camp-fire within two

hundred yards of where I am standing."

He looked sharply around in every direction, but saw nothing of the camp, although positive that his olfactories could not have deceived him.

"Whether it belongs to white or red can't be said, *sartin*; but it's a great deal most likely that it's red, and it's just about as sartin that that Injin ahead of me has gone pretty close to the camp, so I'll keep on follering him."

A short distance further he became assured that he was in close proximity to the fire, and he began to use extreme caution in his movements. He knew very well how slight an inadvertence would betray his approach, and a betrayal was almost fatal. Advancing some distance further, he suddenly came in full view of the camp-fire. He saw three Indians seated around it, smoking, and appearing as if they had just finished their morning meal. It seemed, also, as if they were discussing some matter that deeply interested all. The mumbling of their voices could be heard, and one of them gesticulated quite freely, as though he were excited over the conference. There was not even the most remote possibility that what they were saying was of the least concern to the trapper; and so, after watching them a few moments, he moved cautiously by.

It was rarely that Tim ever had a mishap at such perilous times as these, but to his dismay something caught his foot so dextrously, that in spite of himself he was thrown flat upon his face. There was a dull thump, not very loud, it is true, but he feared it had reached the ears of the savages. He lay motionless, listening for a while, but hearing nothing of their voices or footsteps, he judged that either they had no suspicion of the true cause, or else had not heard him at all. He therefore rose to his feet and moved on, occasionally glancing back, to be sure he was not pursued.

The trapper proceeded in this manner until noon. Had the case been urgent, he would not have paused until nightfall, as his indurated muscles demanded no rest; he could go a couple of days without nourishment, and experience little inconvenience. But there was no call for haste. He therefore paused at noon, on the banks of a small stream, in quest of some water-fowl.

Tim gazed up and down-stream, but saw nothing that would serve as a dinner. He could have enticed a fish or two from their element, but he had set his heart upon partaking of a bird, and was not willing to accept anything else. Accordingly, he began walking down the bank of the creek in search of one.

In such a country as was Minnesota forty years ago, the difficult matter would have been to *avoid* game rather than to find it. The trapper had searched but a short distance, when he caught sight of a single ptarmigan under the opposite bank. In a twinkling Tim's rifle was raised, and, as it flashed forth its deadly messenger, the bird made a single struggle, and then floated, a dead object, down the current.

Although rather anxious for his prize, the trapper, like many a hunter since that day, was not willing to receive a wet skin so long as it was possible to avoid it. The creek could be only of inconsiderable depth, yet, on such a blustering day, he felt a distaste toward exposing himself to its chilling clasp. Some distance below he noticed the creek narrowed and made a curve. At this point he hoped to draw it in shore with a stick, and he lost no time in hurrying to the point. Arrived there, the trapper stood on the very margin of the water, with a long stick in hand, waiting for the opportune moment. He naturally kept his eye upon the floating bird, as

Edward S. Ellis

any animal watches the prey that he is confident is coming directly into his clutches.

From the opposite bank projected a large, overhanging bush, and such was the bird's position in the water, that it was compelled to float within a foot, at least, of this. Tim's eyes happened to be fixed intently upon it at this moment, and, at the very instant it was at the point named, he saw a person's hand flash out, seize the ptarmigan by the neck, and bring it in to shore in a twinkling.

Indignation upon the part of the trapper was perhaps as great as his surprise. He raised his rifle, and had it already sighted at the point where he was confident the body of the thief must be concealed, when a second thought caused him to lower his piece, and hurry up-stream, to a spot directly opposite where the bird had disappeared.

Here he searched the shore narrowly, but could detect no sign of the presence of any person. That there was, or had at least been, one there, needed no further confirmation. The trapper was in no mood to put up with the loss of his dinner, and he considered it rather a point of honor that he should bring the offending savage to justice. That it was an Indian he did not doubt, but he never once suspected, what was true, that it was the identical one he had been following, and who had passed his camp-fire.

In a few moments he found a shallow portion of the creek across which he immediately waded and made his way down the bank, to where the Indian had first manifested his presence. Here the keen eye of Tim at once detected moccasin prints, and he saw that the savage had departed with his prize.

There was no difficulty in following the trail, and the trapper did so, with his long, loping, rapid walk. It happened to lead straight to the northward, so that he felt it was no loss of time for him to do so.

It was morally certain the savage could be at no great distance; hence the pursuer was cautious in his advance. The American Indian would rather seek than avoid an encounter, and he was no foe to be despised in a hand-to-hand contest. The trapper was in that mood that he would not have hesitated to encounter two of them in deadly combat for the possession of the bird which was properly his own, and which he was not willing to yield until compelled to do so by physical force.

About a hundred rods brought the trapper to a second creek of larger size than the first. The trail led directly into this, so he followed without hesitation. Before doing so, he took the precaution to sling his rifle to his back, so that his arms should be disencumbered in any sudden emergency.

The creek proved to be of considerable depth, but not sufficient to cause him to swim. Near the center, when it was up to his armpits, and he was feeling every foot of the way as he advanced, he chanced by accident to raise his head. As he did so, he caught a movement among the undergrowth, and more from habit than anything else, dodged his head.

The involuntary movement allowed the bullet that was discharged at that moment to pass harmlessly over his crown and bury itself in the bank beyond. The next instant the trapper dashed through the water, reaching the shore before the savage could reload. To his disappointment and chagrin, the Indian was gone.

Tim, however, was not to be baffled in this manner, and dashed on as impetuously as before. He was so close that he

Edward S. Ellis

could hear the fugitive as he fled, but the nature of the ground prevented rapid progress upon the part of either, and it was impossible to tell for a time who it was that was gaining.

"There's got to be an end to this race *some time*," muttered Tim, "or I'll chase you up the north pole. You've stole my dinner, and tried to steal my topknot, and now you shall have it or I shall have yours."

For some time this race (which in many respects resembled that of Teddy and the strange hunter) continued, until the trapper found it was himself that was really losing ground, and he sullenly came down to a walk again. Still, he held to the trail with the unremitting perseverance of the blood-hound, confident that, sooner or later, he must come up with the fugitive.

All at once, something upon the ground caught his eye. It was the ptarmigan, and he sprung exultingly forward and picked it up. It was unharmed by the Indian, and he looked upon it as a tacit surrender, on the part of his adversary, of the matter of dispute between them.

At first Tim was disposed to keep up the pursuit; but, on second thought, he concluded to partake of his dinner, and then continue his search for his human game. In order to enjoy his dinner it was necessary to have it cooked, and he busied himself for a few moments in collecting a few dried sticks, and plucking the feathers from the fowl and dressing it.

While thus occupied, he did not forget to keep his eyes about him, and to be prepared for the Indian in case he chose to come back. He discovered nothing suspicious, however, and came to believe there was no danger at all.

At length, when the afternoon was well advanced, the trapper's dinner was prepared. He took the fowl from the blaze, and cutting a piece with his hunting-knife, was in the very act of placing it in his mouth, when the sharp crack of a rifle broke the stillness, and he fell backward, pierced through the body by the bullet of the Indian whom he had been pursuing.

"It's all up!" muttered the dying man. "I am wiped out at last, and must go under!"

The Lost Trail had been the means of Tim, the trapper, discovering what proved to him *the trail of death!*

Edward S. Ellis

CHAPTER IX

THE DEAD SHOT

And now 'tis still I no sound to wake
The primal forest's awful shade;
And breathless lies the covert brake,
Where many an ambushed form is laid.
I see the red-man's gleaming eye,
Yet all so hushed, the gloom profound,
That summer birds flit heedlessly,
And mocking nature smiles around.

—LUNT

Five years have passed. It is the summer of 1825. In that comparatively brief period, what vast changes have taken place! How many have come upon and departed from the stage of life! How many plans, intentions and resolutions have been formed and either failed or succeeded! How many governments have toppled to the earth, and followed by "those that in their turn shall follow them." What a harvest it has been for Death!

The missionary's cabin stands on the Clearing where it was first erected, and there is little change in its outward appearance, save that perhaps it has been more completely isolated from the wood. The humble but rather massive structure is almost impervious to the touch of time. It is silent and deserted within. Around the door plays a little boy, the image of his mother, while some distance away, under the shadow of the huge tree, sits the missionary himself. One leg is thrown over the other, an open book turned with its face downward upon his lap, while his hands are folded upon it, and he is looking off toward the wood in deep abstraction of thought. Time has not been so gentle with Harvey Richter. There are lines upon his face, and a sad, wearied expression that does not properly belong there. It would have required full fifteen years, in the ordinary course of events, to have bowed him in this manner.

The young man—for he is still such—and his little boy are the only ones who now dwell within the cabin. No tidings or rumors have reached him of the fate of his wife, who was so cruelly taken from him four years before. The faithful Teddy is still searching for her. The last two winters he has spent at home, but each summer he has occupied in wandering hither and thither through the great wilderness, in his vain searching for the lost trail. Cast down and dejected, he has never yet entirely abandoned hope of finding traces of her. He had followed out the suggestion of the trapper, and visited the Indians that dwelt further north, where he was informed that nothing whatever was known of the missing woman. Since that time his search had been mostly of an aimless character, which, as we have already stated, could be productive of no definite results.

The missionary had become, in a degree, resigned to his fate; and yet, properly speaking, he could not be said to be resigned, for he was not yet convinced that she was entirely lost to him. All traces of the strange hunter seemed irrecoverably gone, but Richter still devoutly believed the

Edward S. Ellis

providence of God would adjust everything in due time. It is true, at seasons, he was filled with doubt and misgiving; but his profession, his devotedness to his work, brought him in such close communion with his divine Master that he trusted fully in his providences.

On this summer afternoon, thoughts of his wife and of the strange hunter occupied his mind more exclusively than they had for a year past. So constant and preoccupying, indeed, were they, that he once or twice believed he was on the eve of learning something regarding her. While engaged in reading, the figures of his wife and the hunter would obtrude themselves; he found it impossible to dismiss them, so he had laid down the book and gone off into this absorbing reverie.

An additional fear or presentiment at times haunted the mind of the missionary. He believed this hunter who could resort to such diabolical means to revenge himself, would seek to inflict further injury upon him, and he instinctively looked upon his boy as the vulnerable point where the blow would be likely to fall. For over a year, while Teddy was absent, Richter had taken the boy with him, when making his daily visits to the village, and made it a point never to lose sight of him. During these years of loneliness, also, Harvey Richter had hunted a great deal in the woods and had attained remarkable skill in the use of the rifle—an accomplishment for which he had reason to be thankful for the remainder of his life, as we shall presently see. On a pleasant afternoon, he frequently employed himself in shooting at a target, or at small game in the lofty trees around him, until his aim became so unerring that not a warrior among the Sioux could excel him. It may seem singular, but our readers will understand us when we say that this added to his popularity —and, in a manner, paved a way for reaching many a heart that hitherto had remained unmoved by his appeals.

The year preceding, an Indian had presented the missionary with a goat, to the neck of which was attached a large cowbell, that probably had been obtained of some trader. Where the animal came from, however, he had never been able to tell. It was a very acceptable present, as it became a companion for his Charley, who spent many and many an hour in sporting with it. It also afforded for a while a much-valued luxury in the shape of milk, so that the missionary came to regard the animal as an indispensable requirement in his household.

The goat acquired a troublesome habit of wandering off in the woods, with an inclination not to return for several days. From this cause the bell became useful as a signal to indicate the animal's whereabouts. It rarely wandered beyond hearing, and caused no more trouble than would have resulted from a cow under the same circumstances. For the last few weeks it had been the duty, or rather privilege, of Charley to bring his playmate home, and the child had become so expert that the father had little hesitation in permitting him to go out for it. The parent had misgivings, however, in allowing him to leave the house, so near dark, to go beyond his sight if not beyond his hearing; and for some time he had strenuously refused to permit the boy to go upon his errand; but the little fellow plead so earnestly, and the father's ever-present apprehensions having gradually dulled by their want of realization, he had given his reluctant consent, until it came to be considered the special province of the boy to bring in the goat every evening just before nightfall.

The afternoon wore away, and still the missionary sat with folded hands, gazing absently off in the direction of the wood. The boy at length aroused him by running up and asking:

"Father, it is getting late. Isn't it time to bring Dolly home?"

"Yes, my son; do you hear the bell?"

"Listen!"

The pleasant *tink-a-link* came with faint distinctness over the still summer air.

"It isn't far away, my son; so run as fast as you can and don't play or loiter on the way."

The child ran rapidly across the Clearing in the direction of the sound, shot into the wood, and, a moment later, had disappeared from his father's sight.

The father still sat in his seat, and was looking absently toward the forest, when a startled expression flashed over his face and he sprung to his feet. What thus alarmed him? *It was the sound of the goat-bell.*

All of my readers who have heard the sound of an ordinary cow-bell suspended to the neck of an animal, have observed that the natural sound is an *irregular one*—that is, there is no system or regularity about the sound made by an animal in cropping the grass or herbage. There is the clapper's tink-a-link, tink-a-link—an interval of silence—then the occasional tink, tink, tink, to be followed, perhaps, by a repetition of the first-named sounds, varied occasionally by a compound of all, caused by the animal flinging its head to free itself from troublesome flies or mosquitoes. The bell in question, however, gave no such sounds *as these*, and it was this fact which filled the missionary with a sudden, terrible dread.

Suppose a person take one of these bells in his hand, and give a steady, *uninterrupted* motion. The consequence must be a regular, unvarying, monotonous sound, which any ear can distinguish from the natural one caused by the animal itself. It was a steady tink, tink, tink, that the bell in question sent forth.

The missionary stood but a moment; then dashing into the house, he took down his ever-loaded rifle and ran in the direction of the sound. In his hurry, he forgot powder-horn and bullet, and had, as a consequence, but a single charge in his rifle. He had gone scarcely a hundred yards, when he encountered the goat returning home. One glance showed there was *no bell* to its neck, while that ominous tink, tink, tink, came through the woods as uninterruptedly as before.

The father now broke into a swifter run, almost losing his presence of mind from his great, agonizing fear. The picture of the Indian, whom he had felled to the floor, when he insulted his wife years before, rose before him, and he saw his child already struggling in the savage's merciless grasp. Nearer and nearer he approached the sound, until he suddenly paused, conscious that it was but a short distance away. Hurrying stealthily but rapidly several rods to the right, the whole thing was almost immediately made plain to him.

Two trees, from some cause or other, had fallen to the ground in a parallel direction and within a yard of each other. Between the trunks of these an Indian was crouched, who held the goat-bell in his left hand, and caused the sound which so startled the father. The savage had his back turned toward the missionary, and appeared to be looking in the opposite direction, as if he were waiting the appearance of some one.

While the father stood gazing at this, he saw his boy come to view about fifty feet the other side of the Indian, and, as if wearied with his unusual hunt, seat himself upon a log. As soon as the boy was visible, the savage—whom Richter recognized at once as the same man that he had felled to the floor of his cabin, four years before—called into use a little common sense, which, if it had been practised somewhat sooner, must have completely deluded the father and accomplished the design meditated. If, instead of giving the bell the monotonous tink, the Indian had shaken the clapper irregularly, it would have resulted in the certain capture of the child, beyond the father's power of aid or rescue.

The missionary, we say, penetrated the design of the Indian almost instantly. Although he saw nothing but the head and top of one shoulder, he recognized, with a quick instinct, the villain who had felt the weight of his hand years before, and who had now come in the fullness of time, to claim his revenge. Directly in front of the savage rose a small bush, which, while it gave him a view of the boy, concealed himself from the child's observation.

The object of the Indian seemed to be to lure the boy within his reach, so as to secure him without his making an outcry or noise. If he could draw him close to the logs, he would spring upon him in an instant, and prevent any scream, which assuredly must reach the father, who, with his unerring rifle would have been upon the ground in a few moments. It was an easy matter for the savage to slay the boy. It would not have done to shoot his rifle, but he could have tomahawked him in an instant; hence it was plain that he desired only to take him prisoner. He might have sprung upon his prey in the woods, but there he ran the risk of being seen by the child soon enough for him to make an outcry, which would not fail of bringing immediate assistance. His plan, therefore, was, to beguile the little fellow on until he had walked directly into the snare, as a fly is lured into the web of a spider.

This, we say, was the plan of the Indian. It had never entered into his calculations that the goat, after being robbed of her bell, might go home and tell a tale, or that there were other ways in which the boy could be secured, without incurring half the peril he already had incurred.

The moment the father comprehended what we have endeavored to make plain, he raised his rifle, with the resolve to shoot the savage through the head. As he did so, he recalled the fact that he had but a single charge, and that, as a consequence, a miss would be the death-warrant of himself as well as of his child. But he knew his eye and hand would never fail him. His finger already pressed the trigger, when he was restrained by an unforeseen impediment.

While the deadly rifle was poised, the boy stretched himself up at full length, a movement which made known to the father that his child was exactly in range with the Indian himself, and that a bullet passing through the head of the savage could not fail to bury itself in the little fellow's body. This startling circumstance arrested the pressure of the trigger at the very moment the ball was to be sped upon its errand of death.

The missionary sunk down upon one knee, with the intention of bringing the head of the savage so high as to carry the bullet over the body of his boy, but this he found could not be done without too seriously endangering his aim. He drew a bead from one side of the tree, and then from the other, but from both stand-points the same dreadful danger threatened. The ground behind the tree was somewhat elevated, and was the only spot from which he could secure a fair view of the bronze head of the relentless enemy.

Two resorts were at the command of Richter. He could leave the tree altogether, and pass around so as to come upon the savage from a different direction; but this involved delay during which his boy might fall into the Indian's power and be dispatched, as he would be sure to do when he found that the father was close at hand; and from the proximity of the two men, it could hardly fail to precipitate a collision between them. The Indian, finding himself at bay, could not fail to prove a most troublesome and dangerous customer, unarmed, as Richter was, with weapons for a close encounter.

The father might also wait until the boy should pass out of range. Still, there was the possibility of his proceeding directly up to the spot where the savage lurked, thus keeping in range all the while. Then the attempted rescue would have to be deferred until the child was in the hands of the savage. These considerations, passing through Richter's brain much more rapidly than we have narrated them, decided him to abandon both plans, and to resort to what, beyond question, was a most desperate expedient.

The Indian held the bell in his left hand. It was suspended by the string which had clasped the neck of the goat, and, as it swayed gently back and forth, this string slowly twisted and untwisted itself, the bell, of course, turning back and forth. The father determined to slay the Indian and save his son by *shooting this bell*!

It is not necessary to describe the shape and make of the common cow-bell in general use throughout our country; but it is necessary that the reader should bear them in mind in order to understand the manner in which the missionary proposed to accomplish this result. His plan was to strike the bell when in the proper position, and *glance the bullet into the head of the savage*!

The desperate nature of this expedient will be seen at once. Should the gun be discharged when the flat side of the bell was turned toward him, the ball would pass through, and most probably kill his child without endangering the life of the Indian. If it struck the narrow side, it accomplished neither harm nor good; while, if fired at the precise moment, and still aimed but an inch too low, the bell would most likely be perforated. Consequently, it was requisite that the rifle be discharged at the precise instant of time when the signal brass was in the correct position, and that the aim should be infallibly true.

All this Richter realized only too painfully; but, uttering an inward prayer, he raised his rifle with a nerve that knew no faltering or fear, holding it pointed until the critical moment should arrive. That moment would be when the string was wound up, and was turning, to unwind. Then, as it was almost stationary, he fired.

No sound or outcry betrayed the result; but, clubbing his rifle, the father bounded forward, over the trees, to the spot where the Indian was crouching. There he saw him in his death-struggle upon the ground the bell still held fast in his hand. In that critical moment, Harvey Richter could not forbear glancing at it. Its top was indented, and sprinkled with white by the glancing passage of the lead. The blood, oozing down the face of the savage, plainly showed how unerringly true had been the aim.

Something in the upward look of the dying man startled the missionary.

"Harvey Richter—don't you know me?" he gasped.

"I know you as a man who has sought to do me a wrong that only a fiend could have perpetrated. Great Heaven! Can it be? Is this you, Brazey Davis?"

"Yes; but you've finished me, so there isn't much left."

"Are you the man, Brazey, who has haunted me ever since we came in this country? Are you the person who carried away poor, dear Cora?"

"Yes—yes!" answered the man, with fainting weariness.

Such, indeed, was the case. The strange hunter and the Indian known as Mahogany were one and the same person.

"Brazey, why have you haunted me thus, and done me this great wrong?"

"I cannot tell. When I thought how you took her from me, it made me crazy when I thought about it. I wanted to take her from you, but I wouldn't have dared to do that if you hadn't struck me. I wanted revenge then."

"What have you done with her?"

"She is gone, I haven't seen her since the day after I seized her, when a band of Indians took her from me, and went up north with her. They have got her yet, I know, for I have kept watch over her, and she is safe, but is a close prisoner." This he said with great difficulty.

"Brazey, you are dying. I forgive you. But does your heart tell you you are at peace with Him whom you have offended so grievously?"

"It's too late to talk of that now. It might have done years ago, when I was an honest man like yourself, and before I became a vagabond, bent on injuring one who had never really injured me."

"It is never too late for God to forgive—"

"Too late—too late, I tell you! *There!*" He rose upon his elbow, his eyes burning with insane light and his hand extended. "I see her—she is coming, her white robes floating on the air. Oh, God, forgive me that I did her the great wrong! But, she smiles upon me—she forgives me! I thank thee, angel of good—"

He sunk slowly backward, and Harvey Richter eased the head softly down upon the turf. Brazey Davis was no more.

CHAPTER X

CONCLUSION

Heart leaps to heart—the sacred flood
That warms us is the same;
That good old man—his honest blood
Alike we frankly claim.

—SPRAGUE

The missionary gazed sadly upon the inanimate form before him. He saw the playmate of his childhood stricken down in death by his own hand, which never should have taken human life, and although the act was justifiable under the circumstances, the good man could but mourn the painful necessity that occasioned it. The story, although possessing tragic interest, was a brief one. Brazey Davis, as he had always been termed, was a few years older than himself, and a native of the same neighborhood. He was known in childhood as one possessing a vindictive spirit that could never forgive an injury—as a person who would not hesitate at any means to obtain revenge. It so happened that he became desperately enamored of the beautiful Cora Brandon, but becoming aware, at length, that she was the betrothed of Harvey Braisted, the young missionary in embryo, the disappointed lover left the country, and was never heard of by the missionary until he made himself known in the singular manner that we have related at the opening of our narrative. He had, in fact, come to be a sort of monomaniac, who delighted in annoying his former rival, and in haunting his footsteps as if he were his evil shadow. The abduction of his wife had not been definitely determined upon until that visit to the cabin, in the garb and paint of an Indian, when he received the tremendous blow that almost drove the life from his body. Davis then resolved to take the revenge which would "cut" the deepest. How well he succeeded, the reader has learned.

The missionary's child stood pleading for an explanation of the strange scene before him. Loosening the bell from the grasp of the dead man, the minister took the little hand, and, with a heart overflowing with emotion, set out for his cabin. It was his wish to give the hunter a Christian burial; but, for the present, it was impossible. These dying words rung in his ears: "The Indians took her from me, and went up north with her, where she now is, *and safe!*" Blessed thought! She was then living, and was yet to be restored to his arms. The shadow of death passed away, and a great light illuminated his very being. The lost was found!

When the missionary came to be more collected, he concluded that this must be the tribe of which Teddy had once spoken, but which had been visited by him without success. The prize was too great to be intrusted in the hands of another, and Harvey determined to make the search in person, to settle, if possible, once and forever, the fate of his beloved wife.

He soon proceeded to the Indian village, where he left his boy and gave notice that he should not be back for several days. He then called one of the most trusty and skillful warriors aside, and asked for his company upon the eventful journey. The savage cheerfully complied, and the two set out at once. It was a good distance to the northward, and when night came down upon them, many miles yet remained to be passed. There was little fear of disturbance from enemies, and both lay down and slept until daylight, when they were immediately on their way again.

This journey through the northern wilderness was unvaried by any event worthy of record, and the details would be uninteresting to the reader. Suffice it to say that, just as the fourth day was closing in, they struck a small stream, which pursued a short distance, brought them directly upon the village for which they had been searching.

The advent of the Indian and missionary among them created considerable stir, but they were treated with respect and consideration. Harvey Richter asked immediately for the chief or leading man, and shortly stood in his presence. He found him a short, thick-set half-breed, whose age must have been well-nigh three-score years, and who, to his astonishment, was unable to speak English, although many of his subjects spoke it quite intelligibly. He understood Sioux, however, and the missionary's companion acted as interpreter.

Our friend made a full statement of his wife's abduction, years before, and of the assertion of the dying man that she had been taken from him by members of this tribe, who had retained her ever since. The chief waited sometime before replying; he seemed debating with himself as to the proper course to pursue. Finally he said he must consult with one of his warriors, and departed abruptly from the lodge.

Ten minutes later, while the missionary, with a painfully-throbbing heart, was gazing around the lodge, with that minute scrutiny of the most trifling objects peculiar to us at such times, he caught the sound of returning footsteps, and turned to the lodge door. There stood the Indian, and, directly beside him, his own lost Cora!

The next day at noon, a camp-fire might have been seen some miles south of the northern village of which we have made mention. An Indian was engaged in cooking a piece of meat, while the missionary and his reclaimed jewel, sitting side by side, her head reclining upon his shoulder and his hand dallying with her hair, were holding delightful communion. She looked pale and somewhat emaciated, for these years of absence had indeed been fraught with suffering; but the old sweet look had never departed. It was now changed into an expression of perfect joy.

The wife's great anxiety was to reach home and see the child she had left an infant, but who was now a frolicksome boy, and she could hardly consent to pause even when night overtook them, and her lagging limbs told her husband how exhausted she had become. Cora never had suspected the identity of the Indian and the hunter, until on that sad day when he sprung from behind the cabin and hurried her off into the wood. There was something, however, in his look, when he first felt the weight of her husband's blow, that never left her remembrance. While hurrying her swiftly through the wood he said nothing at all, and at night, while she pretended to sleep, he watched by the camp-fire. It was the light of this fire which had puzzled Teddy so much. On the succeeding day the abductor reached the river and embarked in his canoe. A half-hour later he leaned over the canoe and washed the paint from his face and made himself known in his true character, as Brazey Davis, her former lover. He had scarcely done so, when an Indian canoe rounded a bend in the river, and, despite his earnest protestations, the savages took the captive from him, and

Edward S. Ellis

carried her with them to their village, where she had been ever since. Retained very closely, as all prisoners among Indians are, she had heard nothing of Teddy's visit. She was treated with kindness, as the destined wife of a young chief; but the suit for her consent never was pressed by the chief, as it is in an Indian's code of honor never to force a woman to a distasteful marriage. The young brave, with true Indian pertinacity, could wait his time, confident that his kindness and her long absence from home would secure her consent to the savage alliance. She was denied nothing but her liberty, and her prayers to be returned to her husband and child.

At this point in her narration, an exclamation from the Indian arrested attention. All listened and heard but a short distance away:

"Begorrah, Teddy, it's yerself that's entitled to a wee bit of rist, as yees have been on a mighty long tramp, and hasn't diskivered anything but a country that is big enough to hide the Atlantic ocean in, wid Ireland on its bosom as a jewel. The chances are small of yees iver gitting another glimpse of heaven—that is, of Miss Cora's face. The darlint; if she's gone to heaven, then Teddy McFadden don't care how soon somebody else wears out his breeches—that is, on the presumption that St. Peter will say, 'Teddy, me lad, ye can inter an' make yerself at home, to be sure!'"

The husband and wife glanced at each other significantly as the fellow rattled on.

"Wait a moment," said Harvey, rising to his feet, and carefully making his way in the direction of the sound.

It was curious that the Irishman should have paused for his noonday rest in such close proximity to our friends; but, he had learned from a trader who had recently visited the Red

River country, that there *was* a white woman, beyond all question, among the tribe in the north, and he was on his way to make them a second visit.

The missionary found his servant seated by a tree. Teddy looked up as he heard a footstep. It seemed as if his eyes would drop from their sockets. His mouth opened wide, and he seemed, for the moment, confounded. Then he recovered his presence of mind in a measure, and proceeded to scratch his head vigorously. That, with him, ever was a sign of the clearing up of his ideas.

"How do you do, Teddy?" at length the missionary said, after having enjoyed the poor fellow's confusion.

"Faith, but ye sent the cold shivers over me. *Is* it yerself, Mister Harvey, out in these woods, or is it yer ghost on the s'arch for Misthress Cora? I sometimes thinks me own ghost is out on the s'arch without me body, an' I shouldn't be surprised to maat it some day. But I'm mighty glad it's yerself an' not yer ghost, for, to till the thruth, I don't jist like ghosts—they makes a body feel so quare in the stomach."

"Come with me; I have an Indian as company, and you may as well join us."

The Hibernian followed, a few paces behind, continually expressing his astonishment at seeing his master so far away from home. He did not look up until they were within a few paces of the camp-fire, when Richter stepped from before him.

"Save us! save us! but if there isn't the ghowst of Miss Cora come to haunt me for not finding her afore!" exclaimed Teddy, retreating a step or two in genuine terror. "Saint Patherick, Saint Pether, Saint Virgin Mary, protict me! I didn't mane to get dhrunk that day, ye know, nor to make a frind of—"

"I am no ghost but my own self, Teddy, restored to my husband in safety. Can you not welcome me?"

"Oorah! Oorah!" and he danced a moment in uncontrollable joy. Then he exclaimed: "God bliss yer own swate self!" taking her in his brawny arms. "God bliss you! No ghost, but yer own swate self. Oh, I feel like a blast of powder ready to go off!" And again he danced a singular commixture of the jig and cotillion, much to the Indian's amazement, for he thought him crazy. "I knew that I should look upon your face again; but, till me where it is yees have come from?" he finally subsided enough to ask.

Teddy was soon made to understand all that related to the return of the young wife. When he learned that Mahogany, with whom he had so often drank and "hobnobbed," was only the hunter disguised, who was thus plotting his crime, the Irishman's astonishment can hardly be described. He was irritated, also, at his own stupidity. "That Teddy McFadden iver should have been so desaved by that rascal of purgatory!" he exclaimed; but, as the evil man had gone to the great tribunal above, there was no disposition, even in Teddy's heart, to heap curses on his memory.

A few days more, and the three whites passed through the Indian village on their way to the Clearing. The joy of the savages at the return of their sweet, pale-faced sister was manifested in many ways, and she once feared they would never allow her to leave them and go to her own humble home. Finally, however, they reached the Clearing, and, as they walked side by side across it, opened the door and sat down within the cabin, and the fond mother took the darling boy in her lap, the wife and husband looked in each other's faces with streaming eyes, and murmured "Thank God! thank God!"

THE END

Edward S. Ellis

Choose from Thousands of 1stWorldLibrary Classics By

A. M. Barnard
Ada Leverson
Adolphus William Ward
Aesop
Agatha Christie
Alexander Aaronsohn
Alexander Kielland
Alexandre Dumas
Alfred Gatty
Alfred Ollivant
Alice Duer Miller
Alice Turner Curtis
Alice Dunbar
Allen Chapman
Alleyne Ireland
Ambrose Bierce
Amelia E. Barr
Amory H. Bradford
Andrew Lang
Andrew McFarland Davis
Andy Adams
Angela Brazil
Anna Alice Chapin
Anna Sewell
Annie Besant
Annie Hamilton Donnell
Annie Payson Call
Annie Roe Carr
Annonaymous
Anton Chekhov
Archibald Lee Fletcher
Arnold Bennett
Arthur C. Benson
Arthur Conan Doyle
Arthur M. Winfield
Arthur Ransome
Arthur Schnitzler
Arthur Train
Atticus
B.H. Baden-Powell
B. M. Bower
B. C. Chatterjee
Baroness Emmuska Orczy
Baroness Orczy
Basil King
Bayard Taylor
Ben Macomber
Bertha Muzzy Bower
Bjornstjerne Bjornson

Booth Tarkington
Boyd Cable
Bram Stoker
C. Collodi
C. E. Orr
C. M. Ingleby
Carolyn Wells
Catherine Parr Traill
Charles A. Eastman
Charles Amory Beach
Charles Dickens
Charles Dudley Warner
Charles Farrar Browne
Charles Ives
Charles Kingsley
Charles Klein
Charles Hanson Towne
Charles Lathrop Pack
Charles Romyn Dake
Charles Whibley
Charles Willing Beale
Charlotte M. Braeme
Charlotte M. Yonge
Charlotte Perkins Stetson
Clair W. Hayes
Clarence Day Jr.
Clarence E. Mulford
Clemence Housman
Confucius
Coningsby Dawson
Cornelis DeWitt Wilcox
Cyril Burleigh
D. H. Lawrence
Daniel Defoe
David Garnett
Dinah Craik
Don Carlos Janes
Donald Keyhoe
Dorothy Kilner
Dougan Clark
Douglas Fairbanks
E. Nesbit
E. P. Roe
E. Phillips Oppenheim
E. S. Brooks
Earl Barnes
Edgar Rice Burroughs
Edith Van Dyne
Edith Wharton

Edward Everett Hale
Edward J. O'Biren
Edward S. Ellis
Edwin L. Arnold
Eleanor Atkins
Eleanor Hallowell Abbott
Eliot Gregory
Elizabeth Gaskell
Elizabeth McCracken
Elizabeth Von Arnim
Ellem Key
Emerson Hough
Emilie F. Carlen
Emily Bronte
Emily Dickinson
Enid Bagnold
Enilor Macartney Lane
Erasmus W. Jones
Ernie Howard Pie
Ethel May Dell
Ethel Turner
Ethel Watts Mumford
Eugene Sue
Eugenie Foa
Eugene Wood
Eustace Hale Ball
Evelyn Everett-green
Everard Cotes
F. H. Cheley
F. J. Cross
F. Marion Crawford
Fannie E. Newberry
Federick Austin Ogg
Ferdinand Ossendowski
Fergus Hume
Florence A. Kilpatrick
Fremont B. Deering
Francis Bacon
Francis Darwin
Frances Hodgson Burnett
Frances Parkinson Keyes
Frank Gee Patchin
Frank Harris
Frank Jewett Mather
Frank L. Packard
Frank V. Webster
Frederic Stewart Isham
Frederick Trevor Hill
Frederick Winslow Taylor

Friedrich Kerst
Friedrich Nietzsche
Fyodor Dostoyevsky
G.A. Henty
G.K. Chesterton
Gabrielle E. Jackson
Garrett P. Serviss
Gaston Leroux
George A. Warren
George Ade
Geroge Bernard Shaw
George Cary Eggleston
George Durston
George Ebers
George Eliot
George Gissing
George MacDonald
George Meredith
George Orwell
George Sylvester Viereck
George Tucker
George W. Cable
George Wharton James
Gertrude Atherton
Gordon Casserly
Grace E. King
Grace Gallatin
Grace Greenwood
Grant Allen
Guillermo A. Sherwell
Gulielma Zollinger
Gustav Flaubert
H. A. Cody
H. B. Irving
H.C. Bailey
H. G. Wells
H. H. Munro
H. Irving Hancock
H. R. Naylor
H. Rider Haggard
H. W. C. Davis
Haldeman Julius
Hall Caine
Hamilton Wright Mabie
Hans Christian Andersen
Harold Avery
Harold McGrath
Harriet Beecher Stowe
Harry Castlemon
Harry Coghill
Harry Houidini

Hayden Carruth
Helent Hunt Jackson
Helen Nicolay
Hendrik Conscience
Hendy David Thoreau
Henri Barbusse
Henrik Ibsen
Henry Adams
Henry Ford
Henry Frost
Henry James
Henry Jones Ford
Henry Seton Merriman
Henry W Longfellow
Herbert A. Giles
Herbert Carter
Herbert N. Casson
Herman Hesse
Hildegard G. Frey
Homer
Honore De Balzac
Horace B. Day
Horace Walpole
Horatio Alger Jr.
Howard Pyle
Howard R. Garis
Hugh Lofting
Hugh Walpole
Humphry Ward
Ian Maclaren
Inez Haynes Gillmore
Irving Bacheller
Isabel Cecilia Williams
Isabel Hornibrook
Israel Abrahams
Ivan Turgenev
J.G.Austin
J. Henri Fabre
J. M. Barrie
J. M. Walsh
J. Macdonald Oxley
J. R. Miller
J. S. Fletcher
J. S. Knowles
J. Storer Clouston
J. W. Duffield
Jack London
Jacob Abbott
James Allen
James Andrews
James Baldwin

James Branch Cabell
James DeMille
James Joyce
James Lane Allen
James Lane Allen
James Oliver Curwood
James Oppenheim
James Otis
James R. Driscoll
Jane Abbott
Jane Austen
Jane L. Stewart
Janet Aldridge
Jens Peter Jacobsen
Jerome K. Jerome
Jessie Graham Flower
John Buchan
John Burroughs
John Cournos
John F. Kennedy
John Gay
John Glassworthy
John Habberton
John Joy Bell
John Kendrick Bangs
John Milton
John Philip Sousa
John Taintor Foote
Jonas Lauritz Idemil Lie
Jonathan Swift
Joseph A. Altsheler
Joseph Carey
Joseph Conrad
Joseph E. Badger Jr
Joseph Hergesheimer
Joseph Jacobs
Jules Vernes
Julian Hawthrone
Julie A Lippmann
Justin Huntly McCarthy
Kakuzo Okakura
Karle Wilson Baker
Kate Chopin
Kenneth Grahame
Kenneth McGaffey
Kate Langley Bosher
Kate Langley Bosher
Katherine Cecil Thurston
Katherine Stokes
L. A. Abbot
L. T. Meade

L. Frank Baum
Latta Griswold
Laura Dent Crane
Laura Lee Hope
Laurence Housman
Lawrence Beasley
Leo Tolstoy
Leonid Andreyev
Lewis Carroll
Lewis Sperry Chafer
Lilian Bell
Lloyd Osbourne
Louis Hughes
Louis Joseph Vance
Louis Tracy
Louisa May Alcott
Lucy Fitch Perkins
Lucy Maud Montgomery
Luther Benson
Lydia Miller Middleton
Lyndon Orr
M. Corvus
M. H. Adams
Margaret E. Sangster
Margret Howth
Margaret Vandercook
Margaret W. Hungerford
Margret Penrose
Maria Edgeworth
Maria Thompson Daviess
Mariano Azuela
Marion Polk Angellotti
Mark Overton
Mark Twain
Mary Austin
Mary Catherine Crowley
Mary Cole
Mary Hastings Bradley
Mary Roberts Rinehart
Mary Rowlandson
M. Wollstonecraft Shelley
Maud Lindsay
Max Beerbohm
Myra Kelly
Nathaniel Hawthrone
Nicolo Machiavelli
O. F. Walton
Oscar Wilde

Owen Johnson
P.G. Wodehouse
Paul and Mabel Thorne
Paul G. Tomlinson
Paul Severing
Percy Brebner
Percy Keese Fitzhugh
Peter B. Kyne
Plato
Quincy Allen
R. Derby Holmes
R. L. Stevenson
R. S. Ball
Rabindranath Tagore
Rahul Alvares
Ralph Bonehill
Ralph Henry Barbour
Ralph Victor
Ralph Waldo Emmerson
Rene Descartes
Ray Cummings
Rex Beach
Rex E. Beach
Richard Harding Davis
Richard Jefferies
Richard Le Gallienne
Robert Barr
Robert Frost
Robert Gordon Anderson
Robert L. Drake
Robert Lansing
Robert Lynd
Robert Michael Ballantyne
Robert W. Chambers
Rosa Nouchette Carey
Rudyard Kipling
Saint Augustine
Samuel B. Allison
Samuel Hopkins Adams
Sarah Bernhardt
Sarah C. Hallowell
Selma Lagerlof
Sherwood Anderson
Sigmund Freud
Standish O'Grady
Stanley Weyman
Stella Benson
Stella M. Francis

Stephen Crane
Stewart Edward White
Stijn Streuvels
Swami Abhedananda
Swami Parmananda
T. S. Ackland
T. S. Arthur
The Princess Der Ling
Thomas A. Janvier
Thomas A Kempis
Thomas Anderton
Thomas Bailey Aldrich
Thomas Bulfinch
Thomas De Quincey
Thomas Dixon
Thomas H. Huxley
Thomas Hardy
Thomas More
Thornton W. Burgess
U. S. Grant
Upton Sinclair
Valentine Williams
Various Authors
Vaughan Kester
Victor Appleton
Victor G. Durham
Victoria Cross
Virginia Woolf
Wadsworth Camp
Walter Camp
Walter Scott
Washington Irving
Wilbur Lawton
Wilkie Collins
Willa Cather
Willard F. Baker
William Dean Howells
William le Queux
W. Makepeace Thackeray
William W. Walter
William Shakespeare
Winston Churchill
Yei Theodora Ozaki
Yogi Ramacharaka
Young E. Allison
Zane Grey